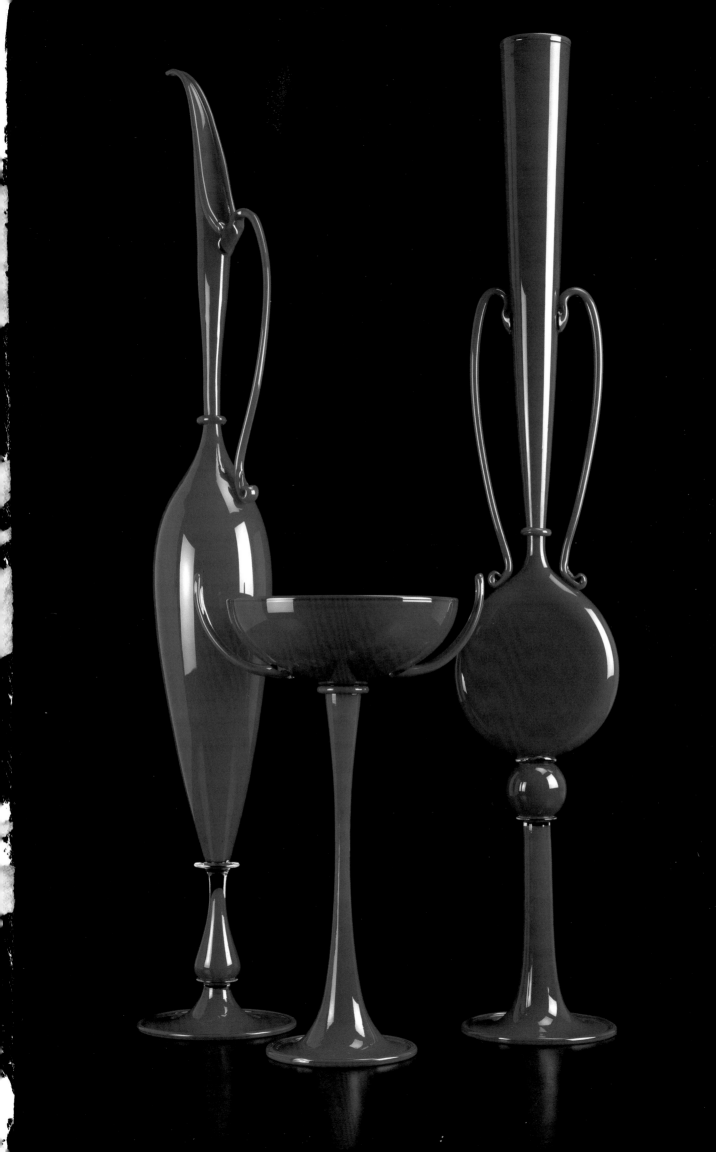

Dante Marioni

BLOWN GLASS

Text by Tina Oldknow

Introduction by Joseph Marioni and Foreword by Edward R. Quick

Photography by Roger Schreiber and Russell Johnson

Distributed by Hudson Hills Press, New York

Library of Congress Cataloging-in-Publication Data
Oldknow, Tina.
    Dante Marioni : blown glass / text by Tina Oldknow ; intro-
    duction by Joseph Marioni and foreword by Edward R. Quick ;
    photography by Roger Schreiber and Russell Johnson.
        p.   cm.
    Includes bibliographical references and index.
    ISBN 1-55595-204-6
    1. Marioni, Dante, 1964– –Catalogs. 2. Art glass–United States–
    History–20th century–Catalogs. 3. Blown glass–United States–
    History–20th century–Catalogs. I. Marioni, Dante, 1964-
    II. Schreiber, Roger. III. Johnson, Russell, 1949- . IV. Title.
    NK5198.M3643 A4 2000
    748'.092–dc21   00-63420

Distributed by Hudson Hills Press, Inc.
1133 Broadway, Suite 1301
New York, NY 10010-8001
Editor and Publisher: Paul Anbinder
Distributed in the United States, its territories and possessions, and
Canada through National Book Network.

Page 1: *Blue Trio*, 2000, greatest h. 40 inches. Collection of the artist.
Page 2: *Mosaic Vase, Green with White Dots*, 1999, 37 × 8 inches.
Collection of the artist.

Project managed by Tina Oldknow
Edited by Jennifer Harris
Designed by Ed Marquand with assistance by Vivian Larkins
Printed and bound by CS Graphics Pte., Ltd., Singapore

NOTE

All dimensions are in inches; height precedes width
precedes depth.

PHOTO CREDITS

Courtesy Benjamin Moore Studio, p. 24; John
Bigelow, N.Y.C. © 1995, p. 38; courtesy The Corning
Museum of Glass, pp. 15, 23, 28; Paul Foster, p. 88;
courtesy Lino Tagliapietra, Inc., p. 25; courtesy The
Los Angeles County Museum of Art, p. 20; courtesy
Paul Marioni, p. 22; Richard Marquis, courtesy
William Traver Gallery, Seattle, p. 27; Tina Oldknow,
p. 13; courtesy The Powerhouse Museum, Sydney,
Australia, p. 76

Contents

Foreword

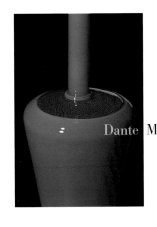

Dante Marioni develops complex glass vessels with such grace that our minds approach them on two levels simultaneously: we are visually drawn by the finely ordered relationships of their component shapes, and we are psychologically awed by the tensions, gradients, and rhythms of their dynamics. His vessel forms are a combination of complexity and simplicity, grouping and counterbalancing volumes so that they flow smoothly into one another. At the same time, he alters the visual rhythm of component forces by subtly redefining their symmetry, therein establishing a whole new tension of elements working dynamically within the object.

Marioni demonstrates a complete mastery of his material, revealing a breadth of training founded upon both classical technique and creativity. His lifelong exposure to glass is like that of a Renaissance artist, learning method and system as a living experience with master glassblowers, and yet he goes far beyond the foundation that underlies his technical proficiency. His creativity is such that he can smoothly make vibrant reinterpretations of classical forms that he understands so well, developing new proportions and hierarchies while retaining ordered relationships. For Marioni, the ancient and traditional are fluid volumes susceptible to redefinition and individual creative vision.

His vessels retain the axes and visual "weight" of ancient forms, the hierarchies of dimension and design that make them appear immediately recognizable. Then the subtleties of his vision come forward: he stretches and reconfigures the volumes of these proportions, creating tensions in

Yellow and Red Pair
1998
greatest h. 40 inches

7

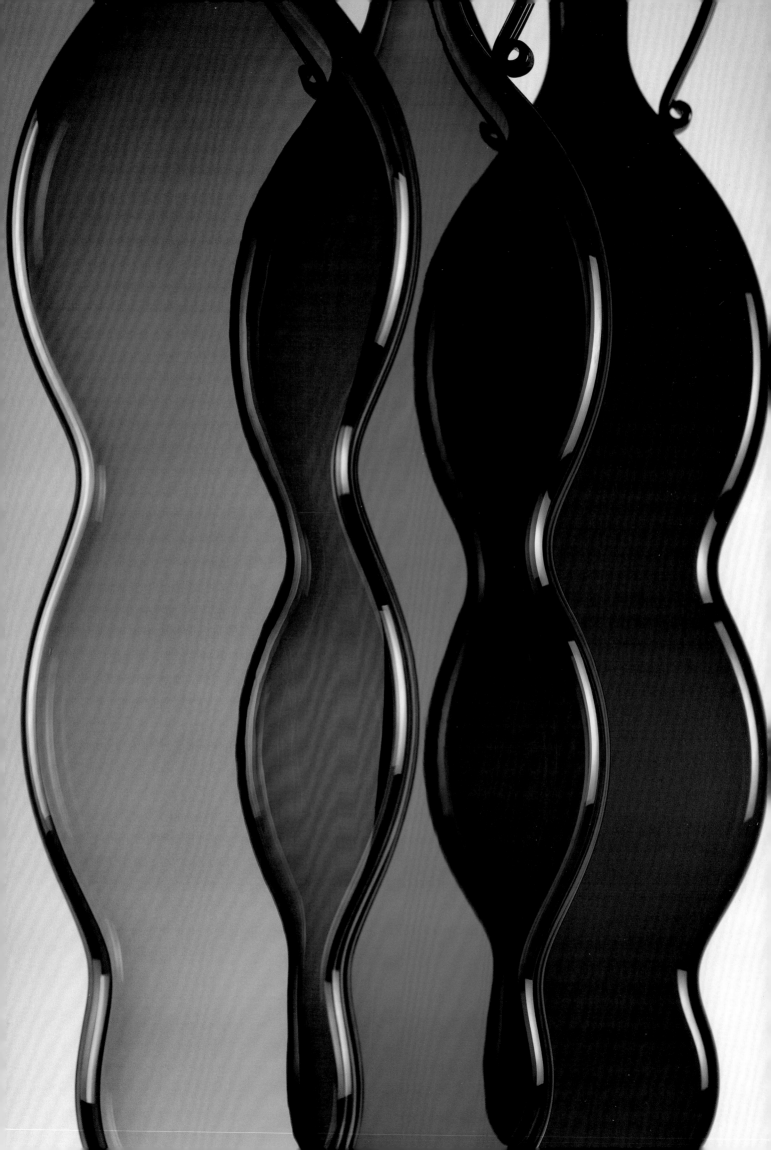

their balance, increasing their verticality, and establishing an entirely new dynamic equilibrium. He passes beyond the preconceived range of formal elements, articulating a new, groundbreaking range of artistic expression.

Marioni's unique combination of classical forms with dynamic, contemporary rhythms is underscored by his use of color to emphasize the intensity of the tensions and resolutions in his vessels. His hues are more than warm or cool colors to enliven forms; they are forceful expressions of the beauty of glass and his dynamic vision of its aesthetic. Color advances and underscores the potency of the vessel in the modern world, at once unique and yet as immediate as the fast-paced society in which it is displayed.

Dante Marioni's skills combine understanding of the foundation of glassblowing, mastery of the possibilities and limitations of his medium, and inspired artistic vision. His finely conceived and balanced vessels are more than formal artistic statements; they are perfectly poised enumerations of directed tension in the medium of glass. Marioni is a master of the sensory and aesthetic effects of redefined form, exploring volumes, tensions, and color, deliberately and with great skill.

detail
Leaf Vases

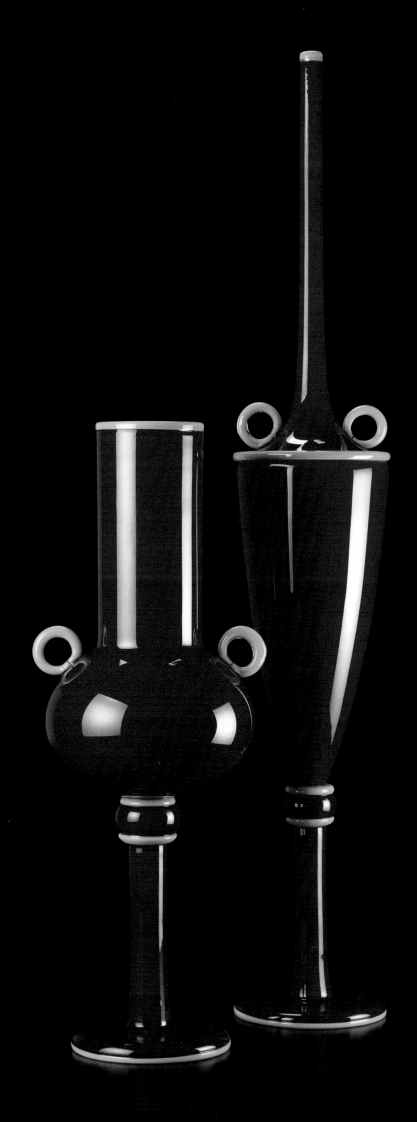

Holding Color

If I asked you to draw a picture of a vessel by Dante Marioni, you could take a pencil and make a general outline of the shape and then fill in the appropriate color. You could show this drawing to someone familiar with the glass world, and they would likely say, "That looks like a Dante Marioni." Your drawing might not capture the volume of the shape or the light of the color, but the drawing as an image of a vessel by Dante would be clearly recognizable. It would be much more difficult to do the same exercise with a group of suspended artifacts by William Morris or a seaform piece by Dale Chihuly.

Drawing a picture of a Morris artifact raises the question of whether your drawing represents Morris's glass or the thing the glass represents. The image identity of Morris's artifacts is involved with being glass and at the same time trying to represent something other than glass. With Chihuly the difficulty lies at the other end of the drawing exercise. How do you draw a picture of a quality of glass itself? Try to imagine a Chihuly seaform piece without its color. The challenge of the drawing exercise would be to represent a flowing surface—linear sheets of glass that are speckled membranes all enveloped within themselves. The difficulty would be to draw the image identity of the form.

The point of this imaginary drawing exercise is to grasp the gestalt identity of the object. This means that we visually see the thing as a complete object and we hold it in our mind as an image. We may not get all the details or the subtlety of the material, but we are capable of drawing its form and representing it as an image.

There is a seemingly simple and unmistakable clarity to the form of Dante's vessels. We can hold in our mind their image identity, the visual gestalt of the object, so that we can picture a vessel—that is, draw a representation of it as a whole image. It is this identity of *holding* that makes Dante's work unique within the glass world. His vessels are not just utilitarian objects to be picked up and used. They are objects to be held in the hand. First of all, his vessels are standing objects, in contrast to things that are hanging or placed at rest. They seem somehow to be related to the human figure, but they are not representations of the human body—although when people do pick them up, they tend to hold them like a newborn baby. Dante's vessels have a direct connection between the eye and the hand that is immediately evident in their form. They seem to be about the pleasure of holding.

During a recent exhibition of Dante's work at the Howard Yezerski Gallery in Boston, a man walked in and asked whether he could pick up one of the pieces and hold it in his hands. He offered, in exchange, to let the gallery hold his credit card. The man was obviously not offering the plastic card as an exchange of aesthetic experience. Ordinary objects in the world have a utilitarian function, and we tend not to look at them until they don't work. Visual works of art, on the other hand, are made to be looked at, and when they are really good we are compelled to look at them. What compels us to look at Dante's vessels is related not only to their visual beauty but also to the truth of their function. It is my contention that the clarity of his form is directly related to his mastery over the craft of making Venetian-style cups and that this gives rise to our desire and our ability to hold Dante's vessels.

To understand how this works, we must first make the distinction between holding something with our fingers and holding something in our hand. We write by holding a pen in our hand, but the delineation of the words is made by the articulation of our fingers. The purpose of holding the pen is for writing. Our fingers are related to line and surface. We use the fingers to verify by touch. The paintbrush is used in easel painting as an extension of a writing instrument to represent a visual narrative. In contrast, the specific holding of things in our hand is related to form. The hand holds other bodies, and we feel their mass and weight.

View of the Grand Canal and the church of San Giorgio Maggiore from
the Palazzo Ducale, Venice.

The concept of "holding" is rooted in the function of "keeping"—to retain and
maintain possession of. To have is to hold.

It is clearly evident that by the mid-sixteenth century, the culture of Venice
focused its creativity on the spectacle of seeing. The Venetians were extremely
concerned with the visual presentation of all aspects of life, and that obsession
with seeing was directly related to the amount and quality of light in their city.
Light was everywhere. It not only came from above and across the sea, but it also
reflected up from the surface of the water that was at their feet. The Venetians'
concept of art was everywhere informed by lustrous and shimmering surfaces.
The Palazzo Ca' d'Oro has a facade of Gothic tracery that was at one time gold-
leafed, and so architectural weight was dematerialized by its delicacy and reflec-
tion on the waters of the Grand Canal. Paolo Pino's explicit inclusion of light in
the concept of color is a major Venetian contribution to Renaissance art theory.
Veronese's paintings are filled with textures of silk and brocades that glisten, and
the virtuosity of Tintoretto's brush drew ribbons of light. The Venetian glass mas-
ters created drinking cups whose primary function is the visual presentation of
the shimmering surface of wine.

Now think for a moment how it is that you pick up and hold a wineglass. Connoisseurs may hold the foot of the glass in their fingers to keep their hand temperature from heating the wine. At the dinner table, you may hold the stem of the glass in your fingers, and if you are standing at a party you might hold the ball of the glass in your hand like a brandy snifter. The brandy snifter is designed to be held in the hand to keep the brandy warm, and it has a small opening that is directed toward the nose. In contrast, the classic Venetian cup is completely open and extremely shallow, like a reflecting pool. A Venetian drinking cup such as we see being presented to us by Bacchus in the painting by Caravaggio is in fact a very difficult thing to drink from. We may delight in the delicacy of the shape of the cup and be amazed by the skill of its craftsmanship; we might even become aware of the play of the two liquids—one frozen in time by the temperature of the air, the other a fluid volume captured in the sheerness of the glass. The function of this cup is for drinking, and yet it is an awkward thing to drink from because it is difficult to keep the wine in the cup. Any movement can easily cause the wine to spill, and you cannot tilt the glass to your mouth—something you might not be aware of if you have never tried to drink from one. The act of drinking was for these Venetians secondary to their obsession with the visual presentation.

These Venetian wine cups are superb examples of a sophist illusion. They are skillfully crafted and can be seductively beautiful, and yet their function is misdirected. When we look at them, the materials and craftsmanship can easily distract us from the logic of their function. We can now see these cups displayed in museum vitrines; they neither have wine in them nor can we pick them up. These drinking cups are directed to the eyes, not the lips.

This brings me to the mastery of Dante's vessels. As objects in the world, they contain, within themselves, a complex gestalt of the identity of holding. It is a simple observation to say that Dante's vessels hold stuff, although I have never seen anything inside one, but then any hollow object can be a receptacle for holding and that alone requires no artistic ability. The observation that I want to make here is that the artistic merit of Dante's vessels is based on his ability to contain technique and create a unity within all aspects of the vessel's function. It is easy

Tazza, Venice, sixteenth century. Blown and mold-
blown glass with gilt decoration. The Corning
Museum of Glass, Corning, New York, 58.3.180.

to recognize an object that does not work, a drinking cup that is awkward to drink from, a tool that we cannot use, a chandelier that doesn't light up. It is, however, very difficult to realize an object that works on several different levels and still maintains the integrity of its intrinsic function. Such things are works of art.

Dante's vessels maintain the integrity of a complex function of holding. This means that beyond his technical knowledge and skill of making the vessel, he has an independent design ability to create an object that holds our attention because all levels of its identity are integrated into its function. What we experience in looking at his vessels is not only the aesthetic pleasure in the relationship of its forms but also the recognition that the form of the vessel is made for the hands. These are not just objects in that we need our hands to pick them up or to verify their texture—we hold them to feel their form and weight. This translates through the eyes into our desire to hold them.

This holding of the object, whether in the hand or in desire, is a shared event between the viewer and the vessel. This can be clearly differentiated from an object whose function is to act as a receptacle to hold the remains of some other event. We look at such objects as artifacts, even if sometimes the other event is only the spectacle of its own making. We can also differentiate the holding identity from objects that are too fragile to be held—objects that despite their open form could not hold anything because the form and material have been stretched nearly to the breaking point. Like a sparkler, they seem to be dissolving before us; their only real function is to dazzle the eyes. It is because such objects are dominated by some other event that we sometimes feel the need to verify their identity by touching. The finger reaches out to touch the texture of a surface, to feel the sharpness of a point, or to trace a lip, but the objects themselves are not made to be held.

Dante makes vessels that hold themselves as complete events true to their function. I think there is no need to put anything in them because the vessels themselves seem to be holding color, and this to me is his extraordinary accomplishment. It is nearly as though you could pick up his vessel and gently turn it over and what would pour out of the mouth is color. Not that the vessel is filled with color, but that it seems as though the vessel is holding color as a part of its being. Note that the vessels are not cast-color, in which the color would be inseparable from the glass, nor is the color applied to the surface of the vessel, and not all the glass is colored. The color is wrapped in clear glass, leaving the color suspended inside the glass itself—not inside the vessel. Dante's vessels are not filled with color; they are literally holding color. So if beauty is truth and truth is beauty, as Keats observed, then Dante's vessels are indeed beautiful, for they display the complete truth of their identity.

Purple and
Chartreuse
Gambo Vases
1997
greatest h. 40 inches

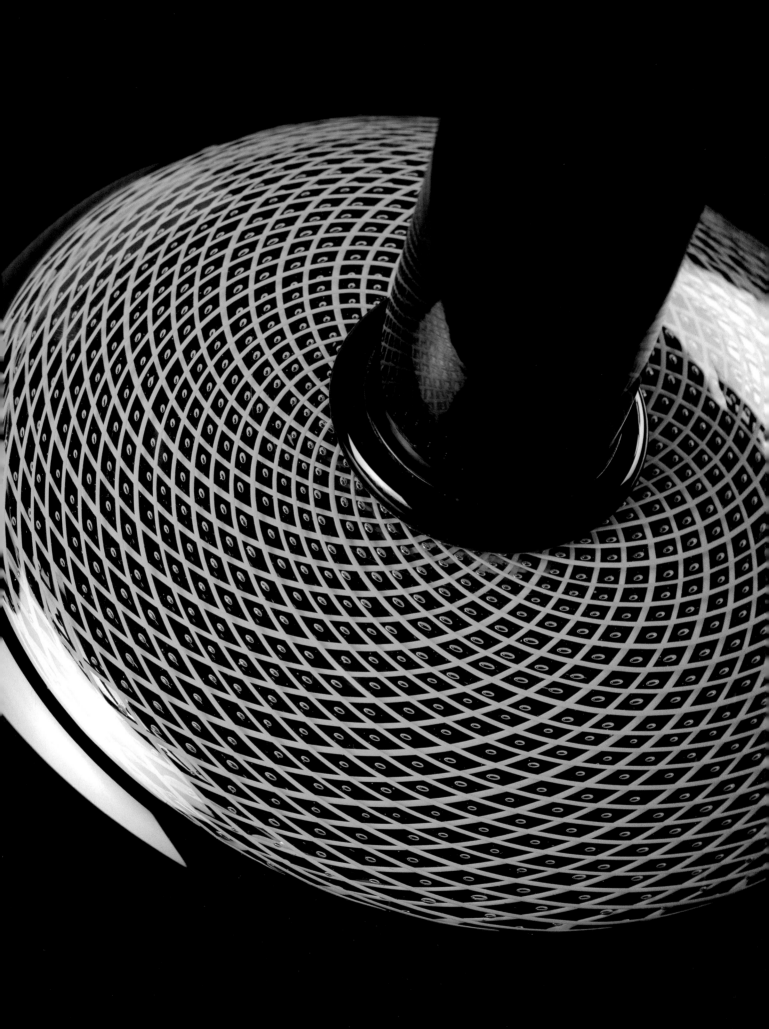

Dante Marioni

GLASSBLOWER

Thou still unravish'd bride of quietness,

Thou foster-child of silence and slow time . . .

O Attic shape! . . .

Thou, silent form, dost tease us out of thought

As doth eternity: Cold Pastoral!

When old age shall this generation waste,

Thou shalt remain, in midst of other woe

Than ours, a friend to man, to whom thou say'st,

"Beauty is truth, truth beauty"—that is all

Ye know on earth, and all ye need to know.

John Keats, *Ode on a Grecian Urn*, 1844

The graceful blown-glass vessels of Dante Marioni are internationally recognized for their intense, vibrant colors and sophisticated, classic design. Marioni has a love and an enduring respect for the process of glassblowing, and he is careful to preserve the traditions of the craft as they were passed on to him. For Marioni, making objects is about the art of glassblowing rather than the blowing of glass art,[1] and his elegant works are the radiant record of his ongoing relationship with the material.

Through the process of making his vessels, which are inspired by forms found in the ancient and Renaissance art of Italy, Marioni has entered a centuries-long artistic conversation about classical design, proportion, and aesthetics that dates back to the first Roman emperors who

detail
Finestra Vase, Black with Yellow and Black Reticello
1999
38 × 8 inches

19

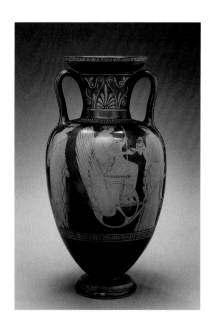

Hector Painter, *Red-Figure Neck Amphora with Triptolemos between Demeter and Persephone*, Attica, Greece, ca. 440 B.C.–430 B.C. Ceramic; h. 17½ inches. The Los Angeles County Museum of Art, Los Angeles, 50.8.23.

looked at Greek art and to the first Renaissance artists who rediscovered classical antiquity. Confident in the strength of his vision and in his mastery of a demanding medium, Marioni has unselfconsciously and studiously pursued his own interpretation of classical design, resulting in forms and colors in glass that are fresh, inventive, and tradition-breaking.

APPRENTICE TO TRADITION

Nobody shall teach glassmaking to anyone

whose father has not known glassmaking.

—Spessart *Ordnung*, 1406

Dante Marioni considers himself a traditionalist, and he has in fact learned glass-blowing in the most traditional way possible.[2] Unlike many artists working in glass today, Marioni is not the product of a college or an art school program. He has learned his craft from American and Italian master glassblowers, primarily the Muranese maestro Lino Tagliapietra and Americans Benjamin Moore and Richard Marquis, both of whom traveled to the Venini glassworks on the island of Murano, near Venice, to learn glassblowing techniques.[3]

Marioni was not a typical apprentice, however. Growing up in a family of influential artists and intellectuals that included his father, Paul Marioni, a pio-neer of the American studio glass movement; his uncle, Joseph Marioni, a painter of monochromatic canvases in New York; and another uncle, Tom Marioni, a performance artist in northern California's Bay Area, the younger Marioni could not help but be aware of movements and trends in contemporary art. More importantly, his world view was shaped by artists, which his naturally questioning, honest, and direct intellect reveals.

A black-and-white photo dating from 1968 shows Dante Marioni as a child with his father in the Mission District in San Francisco. The period is easy for anyone of a certain age to remember: the Bay Area was the center of a counter-cultural revolution, and Haight-Ashbury was the happening hippie mecca. Marioni remembers being with his father and his friends, but he could not appre-ciate what they were doing, being too young to understand the newness of studio glassworking, not to mention their rebellious brand of it. "My father's friends—all artists—definitely influenced me," says Marioni. "I think my education has been from being around all these leaders of the American studio glass movement, like Dick Marquis, who I've known since I was seven years old, Fritz Dreisbach, Jay Musler. . . . It was a big advantage that most people in glass do not have, and I was very lucky."[4]

Richard Marquis, *Teapot and Cozy*, 1973. Blown *murrine* glass
and beaded cozy; 3¼ × 6½ inches.
The Corning Museum of Glass, Corning, New York, 75.4.29.

Marioni was frustrated by the "gooey blobs and drips" that he witnessed being made in the 1970s, but remembers a few pieces from his youth: a Richard Marquis marble, which the artist gave him at a Renaissance Fair, and a Marquis teapot, which interested Marioni mostly because it was nonfunctional. But of all the glass objects lying around the house, the piece that impressed him the most was one made by Benjamin Moore. "My dad had this bowl that Benny had given him, and it was so symmetrical," Marioni remembers. "It looked like a car wheel: it was folded, like a rim on a wheel, and I asked my dad about it, because I hadn't seen anything like it. Everything was dip and drip, that's what I saw growing up in California. I thought it was pretty cool and I looked at it for a long time. It was my favorite thing in the house."[5]

Of all the American studio glass artists who traveled to Venini in the late 1960s and 1970s—Dale Chihuly, Richard Marquis, James Carpenter, Dan Dailey, and Marvin Lipofsky—Benjamin Moore was the one who most absorbed the Venini design aesthetic. As Anna Venini Diaz de Santillana, the daughter of Paolo Venini, has observed, in addition to being a factory, Venini was also a culture, and while disseminating technique to young American artists, Venini's master

Benjamin Moore, *Interior Fold Series*, 1995.
Blown glass; 8 × 28 inches.

glassblowers also disseminated Venini's unique style.[6] Moore returned from Italy with a strong sense of the direction he wanted to pursue in glass, a more design-oriented path that was as foreign to the artists struggling to free glass from its traditional role as vessel as it was to the craftspeople engaged in making popular art glass vases. Moore produced sleek, perfectly round, minimal vessels that were inspired by postwar Italian design, art deco, and turn-of-the-century Austrian glass produced by the Wiener Werkstätte, yet his work remained very contemporary and very American.

In 1979, Marioni's family moved from the Bay Area to Seattle. Dante Marioni began taking lessons at The Glass Eye—a production glass studio started by Seattle artist Rob Adamson—and hanging out in the summer at Pilchuck Glass School with his father, who taught there for fourteen years straight, from 1974 to 1988. For Marioni, Pilchuck was not particularly special because it was a regular, seasonal part of his life. As he remembers it, "Summertime meant Pilchuck."[7] Marioni learned a lot about glass and about working as an artist, and he formed relationships with people who would become very meaningful to him, such as Benjamin Moore and Lino Tagliapietra.

Lino Tagliapietra, *Flute* and *Saturno Goblet*, 1990.
Blown glass *a reticello*; 7 × 5¾ inches.

"I remember going to Pilchuck with my dad in the winter of 1979, when I first started to blow glass," says Marioni. "We went into a studio and there were some objects that Lino had made, all these perfect little cups, bowls, and pitchers. I had never seen anything like it. That's always been something that has intrigued me as a glassblower. I was more interested in perfecting something than in inventing it."[8]

For someone who was not that interested in glassblowing when he started, Marioni caught on quickly, particularly after his graduation from high school in 1982, when he started working full-time at The Glass Eye. It was at The Glass Eye that he first saw Benjamin Moore blow glass, which inspired him to really pursue the craft. "We didn't have any kind of formal mentoring going on, but Benny was the guy I looked up to for everything, in terms of influences," says Marioni. "He was the guy who had the experience, and I listened. Above all, he was friendly to me, and put up with all my questions."[9] Marioni spent most of his time with Benjamin Moore up at Pilchuck, where Moore served as the school's education coordinator from 1974 to 1987.

The year 1983 was a defining one for Marioni. He met Lino Tagliapietra, and he took a glassblowing class at the Penland School of Crafts, taught by the family's longtime friend Fritz Dreisbach. "I don't think that my dad wanted me to pursue [a glassblowing] career," says Marioni. "He wasn't really excited about it when I announced that this was what I was going to do. He just said, 'Really?' ... But after that year, there was no way I was turning back."[10]

Dante Marioni's introduction to Lino Tagliapietra, and Marioni's subsequent development as a glassblower, has acquired a semilegendary quality. "I was there the moment when Dante came up to Pilchuck and saw Lino Tagliapietra," recalls Seattle art patron Anne Gould Hauberg, who founded Pilchuck Glass School with her husband, John Hauberg, and the artist Dale Chihuly. "It is one of the vivid memories I have. Lino was there, blowing glass. And Dante was just nineteen. ... He was standing there and watching, and his face became determined. He was the right age, the right person, at the right place, and in the right circumstances, and he made up his mind, 'I can do that.' You could see it, in his face."[11] "When I saw Lino," affirms Marioni, "that was a big deal. Not to make a huge deal out of one moment, but that was a big deal. After that, every time Lino came back to Seattle, I was present, and my technical abilities changed dramatically each time I was exposed to him. Lino is the master, and that says it all. His command of the glassmaking language is unmatched."[12]

Glassblowing is taught by demonstration, and perfected by endless repetition. In addition to his exposure to Tagliapietra, Dante Marioni was still working at The Glass Eye, where he blew glass every day, all day long, and made goblets in his spare time. He also blew glass in the summers up at Pilchuck, which was the principal place to go for technique during the 1980s. Prior to Lino Tagliapietra's arrival at Pilchuck in 1979, the glassblowing techniques taught there were somewhat idiosyncratic, combining a hodgepodge of European techniques that artists had acquired on their trips abroad, as well as individual preferences. Technique, after all, was not the main priority, and many artists studiously avoided becoming technically proficient until they realized that there was really no other way to get the material to do what they wanted.

Paul Marioni, *The Warriors, Shapers of Our Destiny*, 1984.
Cast glass and steel; 20 × 24 inches.

It is fairly universally agreed that after Tagliapietra's first summer at Pilchuck, glassblowing at Pilchuck (and eventually throughout the United States) was changed forever. "On Lino's second day at Pilchuck, I asked him, 'What do you think?'" Paul Marioni recalls. "Lino said, 'You treat glass like ceramics here, you work it so cold. Glass has to be worked hot.' Lino taught us all the things you could do with glass when it was really hot, and how it had to be worked that way. It was not our generation, but the next generation of glassblowers who learned to blow glass the right way, from the beginning. They had a head start in learning how to do things right, and they quickly surpassed us in technical ability."[13] Dante Marioni was among this new generation. He had blown glass for only a couple of years before veteran glassblowers at Pilchuck started noticing how quickly he was progressing and began to respect his understanding of the craft.

WHOPPERS, ETRUSCANS, NEEDLENOSES, AND TRIOS

*[I am] a foster child of Venice. She has taught me all that
I have rightly learned of the arts which are my joy.*

—John Ruskin, 1877

Dante Marioni, *Whopper Vases*, 1987, greatest h. 24 inches.
This was the announcement photo for Marioni's first
exhibition at Traver/Sutton Gallery, Seattle.

In 1986, the art dealer William Traver offered Marioni his first solo show at Traver's Seattle gallery, giving him a year's advance warning. Marioni knew he had to come up with a new body of work, and he wanted to make it big. So that he could make the larger work, Benjamin Moore offered Marioni the use of his studio on weekends. "This is when I conceived of the *Whopper Vases*," says Marioni. "Benny let me use his shop, and I got the guys together and we set about it. I did not really learn how to blow big from working with the artists in Chihuly's circle. There are little things that you pick up any time you're around glassblowers, but going to Pilchuck and watching Billy Morris blow. . . . Well, Billy does everything himself, because he's a huge guy, and he can reach way out and not get burnt, and I can't. I knew I had to approach it differently. I learned how to blow big by working with people I knew—Benny Moore and Robbie Miller, and my good friends Joey DeCamp, Paul Cunningham, Preston Singletary, and Janusz Posniak, who learned with me."[14]

The primary, comic book colors and heroically scaled, classical shapes of the *Whoppers* (pages 44–46) made an instant, and lasting, impression. No one had ever seen color used in such a way, and on such a scale. The *Whoppers* exploited one of the most ancient forms in glass: the simple flask, which—when handles are added—becomes the classical amphora. The tradition and antiquity of the minimal shape, combined with Marioni's bright, hip, almost pop colors, was irresistible and startlingly original. With the *Whoppers*, Marioni found his aesthetic formula, and it set him on a path of development in form and color with seemingly unending potential. Marioni's art works so well partly because it reflects exactly who he is: Someone who has jettisoned a more free-floating, experimental, "hippie" approach to glass and embraced technique and structure. Someone with a reverence for the past and tradition, who nevertheless is fluent in popular culture.

Marioni began his next series in 1989, when he started to make the *Etruscan Vases* (pages 48–49). The forms were inspired by some ancient storage amphoras Marioni had seen in a magazine. These amphoras, which are commonly found by Mediterranean fishermen, originally were used to ship and store a variety of foods and liquids. They have simple, full, somewhat elongated bodies that are pointed at the base to facilitate burial, up to their shoulders, in cool earth or sand. Marioni paired some of his *Etruscan Vases* with a footed cup, which refers both to the Renaissance Venetian glass *tazza* and to the ancient Greek *kylix*, a two-handled ceramic drinking cup. As with the flask/amphora, it is the handles that distinguish the *kylix* from the *tazza*.

In the following year, Marioni added to his corpus of classical forms, developing a *Goose Beak Pitcher*—a popular Italian shape with Etruscan roots—and a little later, a *Kylix* to go with it. After spending some time perfecting this pitcher-cup duo, which he titled *Pairs* (pages 69, 71, 80–81), Marioni added a third element: a distinctive type of flattened, footed *Flask* (pages 68, 73, 78), which is known as a pilgrim flask. This form also had roots in Renaissance Venetian glass, as well as in ancient Roman glass, and became the final element of what Marioni

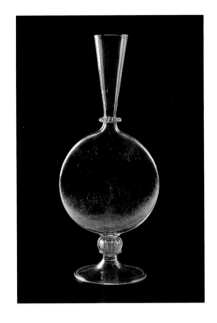

Possibly Vittorio Zecchin, *Pilgrim Flask*, designed 1920s. Blown glass. Collection of Dante Marioni.

Goblet, Venice, late sixteenth or early seventeenth century. Blown glass. The Corning Museum of Glass, Corning, New York, 58.3.194.

called his *Trios* (pages 1, 70, 75, 77, 79). The only other series that Marioni has conceived of in "pairs" are the *Lumpy Pairs*, *Needlenose Pairs*, and *Flask Pairs*, from 1992, 1994, and 1996, respectively. The *Lumpy Pairs* (pages 55–57) — consisting of a ribbed *Pitcher* and *Kylix* — again reference Renaissance Venetian glassblowing techniques and ancient Greek ceramic shapes. The characteristic expanded ribs are used in both Bohemian and Venetian goblets during the late sixteenth century. The technique was also a favorite of Italian glass designer Napoleone Martinuzzi (1892–1977), whose work from the 1920s and early 1930s was instrumental in defining the Italian *novecento* style in glass.[15] For the *Flask Pairs*, Marioni returned to the pilgrim flask form he had first developed for the *Trios*, modifying the proportions so that the *Flasks* were significantly taller and thinner.

Marioni's *Needlenose Pairs* (pages 10, 83–87), in contrast, represent a more personal interpretation of ancient ceramic forms. They are impressive for their synthesis of tradition and innovation, especially since Marioni's understanding of these forms is developed through the process of making the object, rather than the visual analysis of it. The tall, thin neck, stretched out like the jaws of a needlefish, is an interesting modification of the ancient Greek oil bottle, or

Napoleone Martinuzzi, *Amphora with Five
Handles of Grooved Ribbon*, 1930. Blown glass;
h. 13⅜ inches. Il Vittoriale degli Italiani, Prioria,
Stanza della Zambracca, Gardone Riviera

lekythos. The companion pieces to the *Needlenose Vases*, which vary in shape and
size, are more neoclassical than classical, and recall the famous *novecento*-style
vases designed by Napoleone Martinuzzi. As Marioni is quick to point out, the
combination of his forms is historically inaccurate, but this fact makes them even
more interesting. Marioni's ability to take ancient forms and combine them with
each other or with later, neoclassical interpretations, or even significantly modify
them and still have them feel classical, is partly what makes his work so original.

In 1999, Marioni introduced a "new style" of *Trios* (pages 82, 93–94, 96),
which presented taller, thinner silhouettes of the *Goose Beak Pitcher*, *Kylix*, and
Flask. As he has refined his blowing ability over time, Marioni has gradually
moved away from shorter, fuller forms to more elongated, almost mannerist ones.
Marioni maintains that the thinner shapes were what he was always striving for,
but that he just did not have the skill to make them. A look at the artist's drawings from a few years ago shows, indeed, that Marioni's newer forms are closer to
the drawn profiles. "I'm constantly having ideas to make things that are technically beyond where I'm at," says Marioni. "There are a lot of things that I want to
do that I simply can't pull off now. So, I just keep working at it until I get it."[16]

COLOR, LEAF VASES, AND MOSAICS

Everyone knows that yellow, orange, and red suggest ideas of joy and plenty.

—Eugène Delacroix (1798–1863)

Dante Marioni's intense, saturated colors are as stylish as his forms are classic. His combination of opaque colors and classical forms has some relation to the Italian *novecento*-style vases produced by designers like Napoleone Martinuzzi and Tomaso Buzzi (1900–1981), yet Marioni's color sensibility remains very personal and very American in its references to American popular culture. Opaque colored glasses ultimately have their precedent in the ancient and Renaissance glasses made in imitation of gems and semiprecious stones, and have been, over the course of centuries, a Murano staple.

Marioni has no color theories, but bases his choices on what looks good together and what colors will be most compatible.[17] He enjoys shopping for color, and approaches the purchase of colors in the same way he shops for produce—he looks at everything and chooses what looks good. Standing in Marioni's studio, in fact, is not unlike standing in the midst of a large outdoor farmers market, with its vistas of appealing colors in a variety of round shapes. Marioni is inspired by the colors he finds, and the availability of colors on a given shopping day will dictate what he uses in his work. Colors change, often dramatically, from batch to batch, and when Marioni finds the perfect egg-yolk yellow or clear gray, he will make as much use out of it as he can.

"My uncle Joe has influenced me, but not directly," notes Marioni. "He paints monochrome color fields—just a square of blue or yellow—and he rolls the paint onto the canvas, he doesn't use a brush. His finished pieces are stunning, and I like that kind of impact."[18] Marioni observes that his own use of color is "too minimal for most people" and that his work, in many ways, is a reaction to intense surface decoration. The art glass of the 1970s was characterized by a penchant for fuming, which created an iridescent, Tiffany-style surface, while in the 1980s, glassblowers favored the application of additional color in the form of "jimmies" (small bits of colored glass) and internal decorations such as Venetian *filigrana* techniques. Marioni learned all these techniques during his employment at The Glass Eye, whose production glasswares were highly decorative.

Following his instinct for the concentration of color that wears best on his forms, Marioni has stuck with opaque colors, with occasional forays into more transparent hues. He admires other people's use and understanding of transparent colors—particularly that of Seattle artist Sonja Blomdahl and Italian artist Laura de Santillana—but using transparent colors, for him, is a quite different process. Mainly, he cannot shop for transparent colors the way he shops for opaque (because the transparent rods are uniformly dark), and thus he must go after something he already has in mind instead of being inspired by a new color. Yet certain pieces seem to take transparent colors well, particularly the *Leaf Vases*, begun in 1994. This series, and the *Mosaic Vases*, begun in 1996, are Marioni's only nonopaque colored series. "I have also blended colors, transparent and opaque," adds Marioni. "But I realized after making some of the pieces— like the *Whopper Vases*—that the transparent colors didn't work with the static shapes I was doing. The straight lines did not do as well as more curving ones, for example."[19]

The *Leaf Vases* (pages 8, 51–53), which gave Marioni plenty of curves to work with, seem at first to represent something of an anomaly in Marioni's work. "I started making them when I visited the Rhode Island School of Design in 1993," says Marioni. "I made little colorless maquettes and started making large pieces shortly thereafter. They don't really refer to anything other than a leaf, yet they have elements that derive from Venetian glass."[20] What Marioni particularly likes about the *Leaf Vases* is the repetitive curve of their profile, which translates well in both opaque and transparent colors.

The *Mosaic Vases* (pages 98–123)—large, minimal, tall-necked forms that relate to the *Whoppers*—were started as a project with Richard Marquis during a workshop in Japan. Both Marquis, a master of the Venetian *murrine* (mosaic) technique, and Marioni wanted to re-create a specific kind of *murrine* called *occhi* (eyes), which employed colorless *murrine* ringed with a solid color, such as black, red, or yellow.[21] Marioni recalls that the first *occhi* piece he and Marquis made was "black with little clear windows." From Japan, the two artists continued to Australia and made more of them. "We made one with red and yellow checkerboards," says Marioni, "and the following spring, we brought a whole bunch of color bars to Pilchuck and made all these experimental pieces. It was really special for me to be able to do that."[22]

The *Mosaic Vases*, like the *Leaf Vases*, represented a different path for Marioni. For the first time, he used colorless glass combined with solid colors for his huge forms—a radical departure from his opaque colors—and even more unexpectedly, opened himself up to the idea of internal decoration. Although Marioni had long made work with and for other people that involved all kinds of internal decoration and other "surface embellishments," he had not applied them to his own work.

GOBLETS, GAMBOS, AND FINESTRAS

Considering its brief and short life owing to its brittleness, [a glass]
cannot and must not be given too much love. And it must be used and kept
in mind as an example of the life of man and of the things of this world,
which, though beautiful, are transitory and frail.

−Vannoccio Biringuccio, *De la Pirotechnica*, 1540

Dante Marioni, *Green Chandelier*, 1999.
About 120 × 24 inches. Ninth and
Broadway Building, Tacoma, Washington.

Dante Marioni's understanding of traditional forms ultimately stems from his reverence for them. The goblet in particular has been a focal point for Marioni, not
only because goblets are the best glassblowing "exercise," but also because they
represent a perfect glass form. While footed cups are known in ancient Roman
glass, the true goblet, a form that embodies the fundamental Renaissance ideals
of harmony, proportion, and balance, was a Muranese invention.[23] Goblets have
been an interest of Marioni's ever since he worked at The Glass Eye and, later,
with Richard Marquis, whom he assisted in making the *Teapot Goblets*. Although
Marioni's goblets do not have a whole lot to do stylistically with his larger and
more colorful work (at least not prior to 1997), they are what he tends to make for

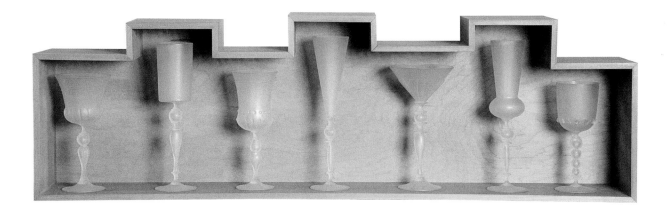

Dante Marioni, *Cup Shelf #4*, 1996.
W. 40½ inches. Collection of Chap and
Eve Alvord.

himself. It is as if the goblet acts as a point of departure for Marioni—those small,
demanding shapes, almost always made in colorless glass, that bring his attention
back to the material.

Marioni has taken some interesting detours with goblets (pages 90–91), resulting in collections of them presented in boxes or forming a gigantic column,
such as his recent chandelier for an office building in Tacoma, Washington, made
entirely of transparent green goblets. Marioni conceived of his boxed presenta-
tions as an "homage to the goblet," setting aside goblets he had made and particularly liked for his "collections." One of these projects consisted of a series of
goblets lined up and fitted inside a box that had been designed around their proportions. Marioni liked the "skyline" effect made by the cup shelf, and had the
goblets sand-blasted and acid-etched so that they would show up better. "It was
about goblet appreciation, to me, in a custom display unit," says Marioni. "Like
the other cup projects I've done, I originally made it for myself."[24]

Marioni's ultimate homage to the goblet, however, may be the *Gambo Vases*,
which he started making in 1997. The *Gambo*, or "leg" in Italian, refers to the
simple type of blown goblet stem that was Marioni's source for the new form. "The

Dante Marioni, *Goblet*. Detail of the stem, showing
the source for the shape of the *Gambo Vase*.

stem of a Venetian goblet is a drip," explains Marioni. "It's a bubble that the glassblower just lets drip, and there's nothing more natural than that in glassblowing.
That's where the *Gambo Vases* come from: the stem. It's a natural form for glass."[25]

The *Gambo Vases* (pages 17, 58–67) are elegant, almost bowling pin–like
forms that are essentially two big bubbles joined using an *incalmo* technique.
Unlike Marioni's other large vessels in opaque colors, the *Gambos* are not primarily one color with a second accent color used to articulate handles, balls, and
wraps, but are instead two vivid colors that interact in an entirely different way.
There are many precedents for the use of the *incalmo* technique, and works of
particular interest to Marioni include pieces by the Finnish designer Tapio
Wirkkala (1915–1985), whose 1960s *incalmo* designs for Venini are well known,
and Seattle glassblower Sonja Blomdahl, who uses double and triple *incalmo*
joins in her vessels. Through his use of *incalmo*, Marioni has further integrated
his forms and colors, and as a result, color plays a larger role in visually defining
the form. The *Gambos* are dynamic, contemporary shapes that, although historic, have become abstracted and ahistoric through Marioni's manipulation of
scale and reduction of form.

Tapio Wirkkala, *Incalmo Bubble Bottle*, designed
1966. Blown glass; 9 × 5 inches. Collection of
Dante Marioni.

After his initial involvement with surface decoration in the *Mosaics*, Marioni
has recently returned to this idea with his *Finestra Vases* (pages 125–39), a series
begun in 1999. Starting with a basic *Gambo* shape, Marioni has introduced a
"window," or *finestra*, at the shoulder of the vessel that is executed in mosaic (the
same technique used for the *Mosaic Vases*) and, most recently, in the Renaissance
Venetian *filigrana* technique known as *a reticello. Vetro a reticello* is a type of
internal decoration in which air bubbles are trapped within a net pattern. The
technique—which looks impressive and is, in fact, challenging—usually features
tiny bubbles and thin netting, and it is primarily used for plates and goblets.
Marioni's *reticello*, on the other hand, is considerably magnified. The netting
is closer to the size of a fishing net, rather than a hairnet, and the bubbles are
correspondingly larger. At this size, there is no room for mistakes: everything is
noticeable, and the placement of bubbles has to be perfect.

With the *Finestras*, Marioni has found an original way to incorporate internal decoration without disrupting his minimal forms—not an easy feat. Again, the
Finestras are interesting not only for the interpretation of traditions that they represent, but also for the personal, innovative way in which Marioni has translated

Dante Marioni, *Yellow Pair*, 1993.
Greatest h. 31 inches. White House
Collection, Washington, D.C.

and even redefined those traditions. While Marioni maintains that he feels more comfortable, as a glassblower, in the realm of design rather than art,[26] it is this aspect of his work that distinguishes it as art, which the best design always is.

A final, significant aspect of Dante Marioni's work is the monumentality and architectonic quality of his vessels. This is unusual to find in blown glass, and is partly a consequence of Marioni's classicism. Certainly, Marioni's tall, thin pieces reference urban architecture in their scale and verticality, but even the smaller vessels have an undeniably architectural feel. This is most evident when Marioni's objects are positioned against an architectural backdrop, such as the photograph of the *Yellow Pair* that appeared on the cover of *The White House Collection of American Crafts*.[27] In that photograph, the *Pair* is shot in the context of an antique American interior, that of the White House, with a view of the Washington Monument beyond. The soaring spout of the *Goose Beak Pitcher* echoes the ascent of the obelisk, while the horizontal profile of the *Kylix* is repeated in the skyline of the Mall's uniformly high buildings, establishing a surprising and breathtaking visual relationship between the forms. Hopefully, Marioni is proud of that photograph. Rarely does such a harmony between architecture and art, particularly functional forms, assert itself. Then again, rarely does such a reverence for tradition and process as Marioni's result in a direction for art so individual, unselfconscious, and untraditional.

NOTES

1. Rika Kuroki, "Interview with Dante Marioni," *Glass Works*, January 1990, p. 60.

2. This section title is taken from the article by Seattle art critic Matthew Kangas, "Dante Marioni: Apprentice to Tradition," *American Craft*, February/March 1994, pp. 34–37. The Spessart *Ordnung* was a compilation of rules and policies for glassmakers of the forest of Spessart in northern Germany and was first written down in 1406.

3. Paolo Venini (1895–1959) was the founder of the influential Venini glassworks on Murano. His son-in-law, Ludovico Diaz de Santillana (1931–1989), ran the company until 1985, when the glassworks passed out of family hands.

4. Kuroki, *Glass Works*, p. 61.

5. Dante Marioni, author interview, November 1999.

6. Anna Venini Diaz de Santillana, author interview, June 1997. After earning his M.F.A. from the Rhode Island School of Design, where he had worked with James Carpenter and Dale Chihuly, Moore went to Venini in 1978 and again in 1979, where he had the opportunity to work closely with Checcho Ongaro. See Ron Glowen, "Benjamin Moore: On Center," *Glass Magazine*, March 1992, pp. 31–35, and Victoria Milne, "Conversation with Benjamin Moore," *Glass Magazine*, summer 1994, pp. 12–16.

7. Dante Marioni, author interview, April 1995.

8. Dante Marioni, author interview, November 1999.

9. Ibid.

10. Dante Marioni, author interview, November 1999, and Kuroki, *Glass Works*, p. 60.

11. Anne Gould Hauberg, author interview, August 1994. I heard the story of their encounter from many of the people I interviewed for my book on Pilchuck Glass School, and it is clearly one of Pilchuck's historic moments.

12. Dante Marioni, author interview, November 1999, and Kuroki, *Glass Works*, p. 60. Lino Tagliapietra's education in glass followed a path relatively unchanged since the fourteenth century, something possible only in Murano. He began blowing glass at the age of eleven, as an apprentice to the internationally known Muranese master Archimede Seguso, and by age twenty-two—rather young by Muranese standards—had earned the important title of maestro. Over the next two decades of his career, Tagliapietra was associated with several famous Muranese glass firms, including Venini, where he worked mainly to observe the famous master Mario "Grasso" Tosi in action. In the late 1970s, Tagliapietra began his influential collaborations with foreign artists, and his own metamorphosis from master glassblower, to designer, to internationally recognized artist.

13. Paul Marioni, author interview, August 1994.

14. Dante Marioni, author interview, November 1999.

15. Inspired by decorative arts movements in Austria and France, like the Wiener Werkstätte and particularly art deco, the *novecento* style in glass celebrated dynamic geometric and curving silhouettes, as well as stylistic references to historical glass.

16. Kuroki, *Glass Works*, p. 61.

17. Until recently, Marioni used only Kugler color rods, which are made in Germany. Problems with color that most people working in glass today experience have to do with compatibility: often colors are incompatible with each other, or incompatible with colorless glass. Incompatibility eventually results in breakage, and artists have tried to subvert this in the past by using only certain color combinations or by working with higher-compatibility Italian colors. Bullseye Glass, in Portland, Oregon, recently introduced a line of wide-ranging colors that are compatible with each other and with colorless glass. Many artists, including Marioni, have started to use the new Bullseye colors.

18. Dante Marioni, author interview, November 1999, and Kuroki, *Glass Works*, p. 61.

19. Dante Marioni, author interview, November 1999.

20. Ibid.

21. This technique was pioneered in Murano by the glass designer Tobia Scarpa (b. 1935), son of the famous architect and glass designer Carlo Scarpa (1906–1978).

22. Dante Marioni, author interview, April 1997.

23. The Renaissance goblet represented a new form for glass that was not derived from shapes found in metalwork or ceramics. This new style of glass had a tremendous impact throughout the Renaissance world, increasing the demand for Venetian glass and ensuring continued prosperity for the glass manufacturers of Murano.

24. Dante Marioni, author interview, November 1999.

25. Ibid.

26. Nola Anderson, "Anatomy of the Vessel," *Craft Arts*, October/December 1987, p. 72.

27. Michael W. Monroe and John Bigelow Taylor, *The White House Collection of American Crafts*, New York: Harry N. Abrams, 1995.

Plates

A lot of times, people have said how Italian my work seems to be. I also hear, almost as much, that people think what I do is very American. In a way, it's Italian-American, because I'm trying to make something that's age-old technically but is American in its boldness. I've been influenced more by American artists, the pioneers of the studio glass movement, than I have by anyone else. This is not to discount the enormous impact Lino Tagliapietra has had on my work.

Colored Cups
1994
greatest h. 8 inches

Whopper Vases
1992
greatest h. 27 inches

Whopper Vases
1993
greatest h. 28 inches

Prior to my first show at Traver/Sutton Gallery (now William Traver Gallery) in 1987, I was working as a production glassblower at The Glass Eye in Seattle. I made goblets and just kind of goofed around. The *Whoppers* were the first pieces that I called my own.

Whopper Vases
1992
greatest h. 27 inches

For the Etruscan Vases, making the handles was the challenge. I remember looking at an article in *National Geographic* about the excavation of an ancient shipwreck off the floor of the Mediterranean. The archaeologists had pulled up lots of ceramic pots—they were pointed amphoras, with no feet. I really liked those forms.

Chartreuse Etruscan Pair
1989
greatest h. 37 inches

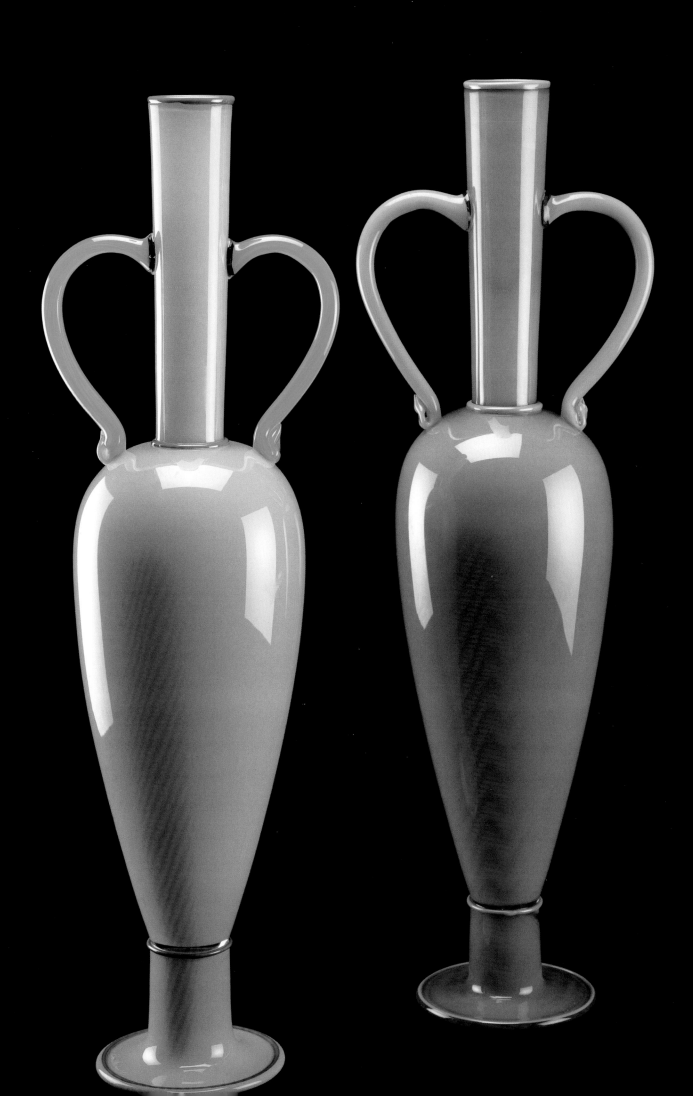

I like the leaf form. I like the way it's done in 1950s wallpaper or
those kitschy 1950s ceramic dishes, and I have always ad-
mired the leaf bowls and plates Tyra Lundgren made for
Venini. The *Leaf Vases* are the most unusual form I've made.
They have historical references like my other work, but
they don't really refer to anything other than a leaf. There's
no direct reference to nature in anything else I've made,

Leaf Vases
1998
greatest h. 45 inches

I started making the *Leaf Vases* in transparent colors. All the
transparent color bars look the same—they are all dark.
Normally, when I shop for colors I react to the colors that I
see on the shelf. Working with transparent colors, I have to
know what I want beforehand, rather than being able to
pick out colors that inspire me.

The ribbed pitchers probably ultimately come from hanging around Dick Marquis and looking at what he calls his "lumpy" forms. The style of the mouth is what the Italians call a "priest's hat." There's a small, perfectly blown, clear pitcher with a mouth like this up in the lodge at Pilchuck Glass School. Lino Tagliapietra made it in 1979, during his first visit there, and that's where I first saw this kind of mouth and neck. I added the ribbing. I particularly like the chartreuse one. It just holds a note, the form does—I hit it right. I like the proportions; I like everything.

Chartreuse Pair
1992
greatest h. 32 inches

➤

Red Pair
1992
greatest h. 33 inches

Orange Pair
1992
greatest h. 32 inches

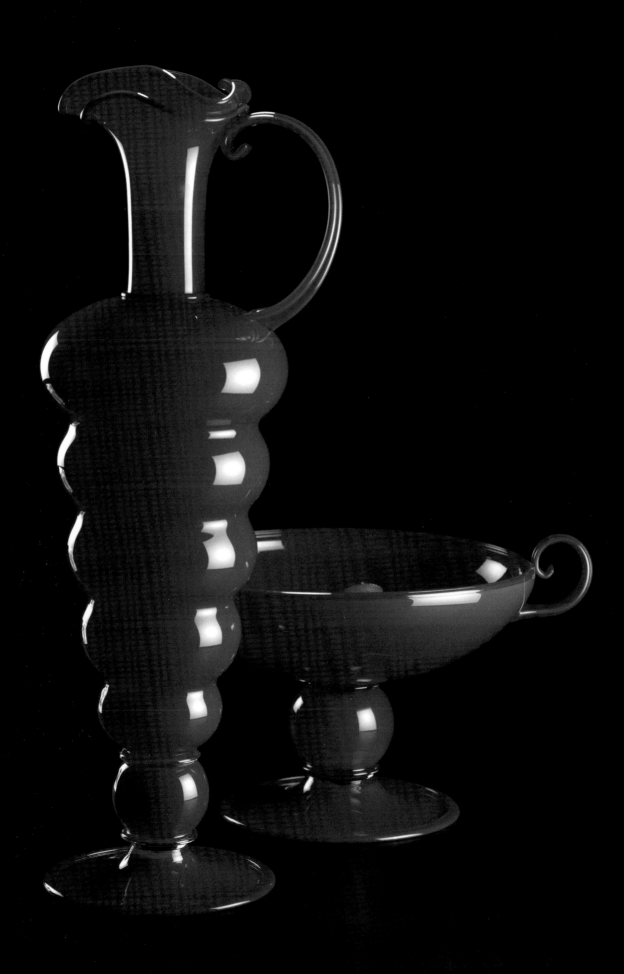

Red and Yellow
Gambo Vases
1998
greatest h. 41 inches

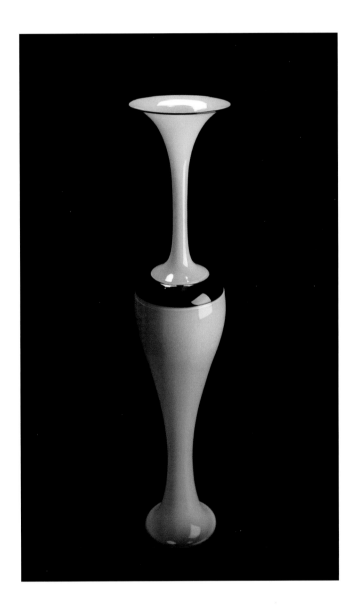

Yellow with Black Gambo Vase
1998
40 × 8 inches

The Gambo Vases *are really difficult.* They're tall, skinny, and large, and they're the most stressful to make. The whole thing can get off-center really badly while we're working it, and I can't really tell what it will look like until it comes out of the annealer.

Gambo Vases
1998
greatest h. 39 inches

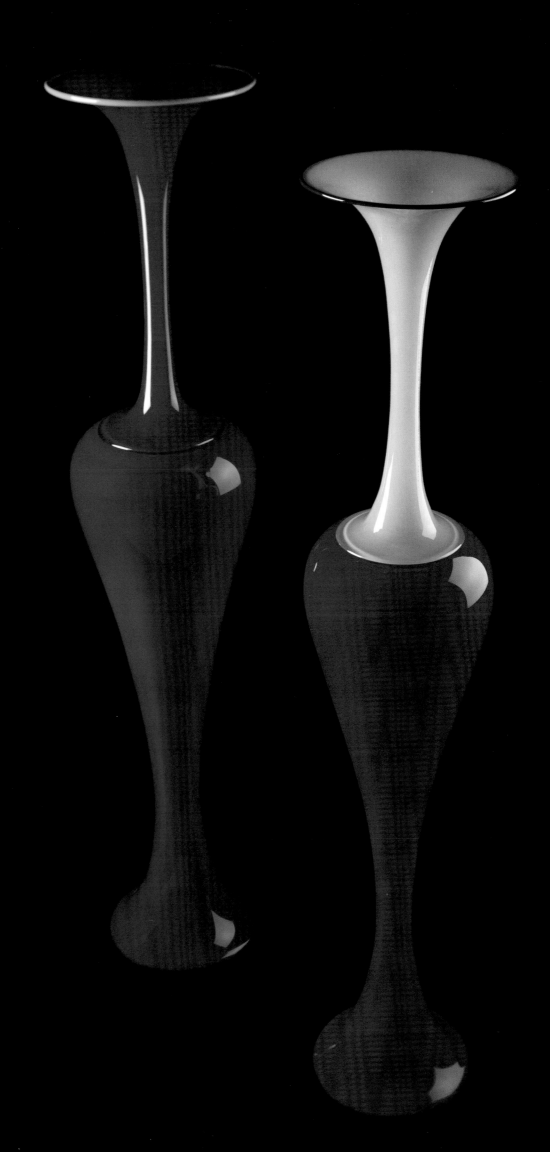

I have only one shot at perfectly joining the bubbles. Joining up really big is much harder to do than just attaching a straight neck onto the body of a vase. The *Gambo Vases* are difficult to make, in every way.

detail
Gambo Vase

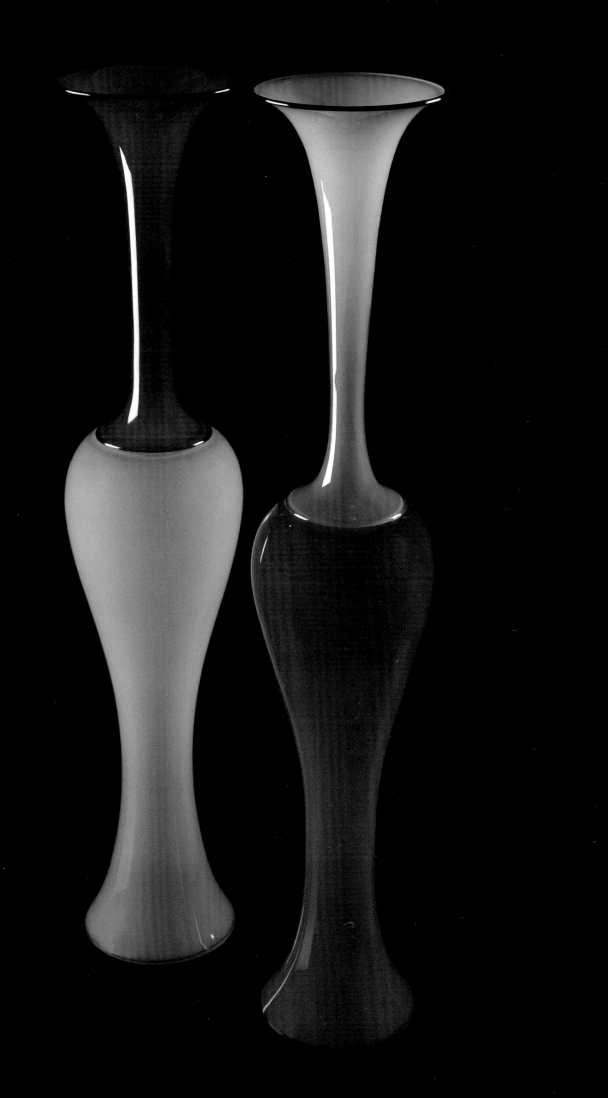

I started blowing glass and discovered that I liked tall and thin
forms, and my pieces have gradually gotten that way. When
I make drawings, that's the way they come out: tall and thin.
It can take me several years before I am able to make what
I have drawn. My eye has evolved too. Looking at slides of
my early work, I remember that at the time I thought my
vessels were perfect. Now I look at this work and I see that
I'm much better today at what I do.

Blue and Red
Gambo Vase
1998
39 × 8½ inches

Rhubarb and Milfoil
Gambo Vases
1996
greatest h. 35½ inches

Pea Green Pair
1999
greatest h. 39 inches

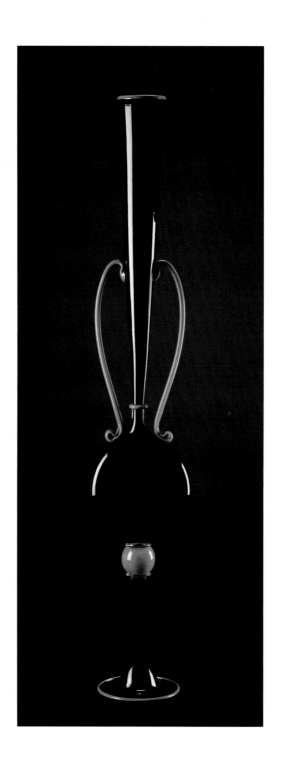

Black and Green Flask
1998
48 × 8 inches

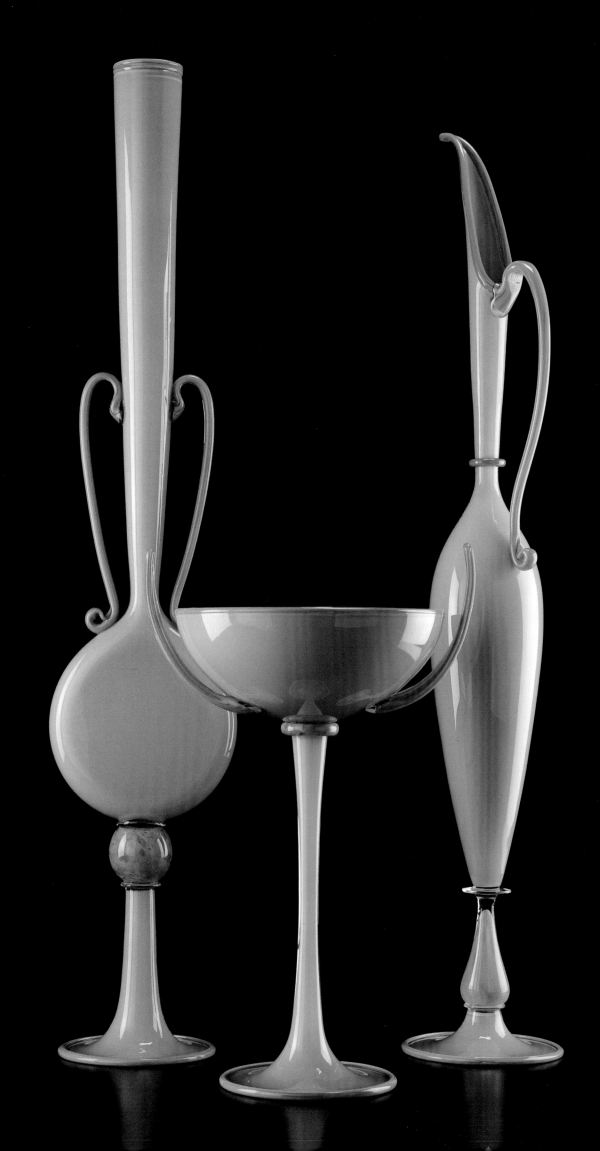

Chartreuse and Orange Pair
1996
greatest h. 38½ inches

For the groupings, I developed the *Goose Beak Pitcher* first. I always thought that it would need a companion, like a bowl, and that form came along about a year later. I tend to work on one object at a time and focus all my energy on learning how to make a particular piece before I move on to the next one. The *Flask* came later. I love the shape of the Venetian pilgrim flasks, and it just seemed naturally to go with the other two forms.

Flask Pair
1996
greatest h. 40 inches

I always wanted to focus on form, and I was inspired by depictions of sixteenth- and seventeenth-century Italian glass that I saw in Old Master paintings, like those by Caravaggio, or in Dutch still lifes.

New Blue Trio
1997
greatest h. 34 inches

Ivory Pair
1996
greatest h. 35 inches

Pea Green Trio
1998
greatest h. 36 inches

78

Oxblood Flask
1998
50 × 8 inches

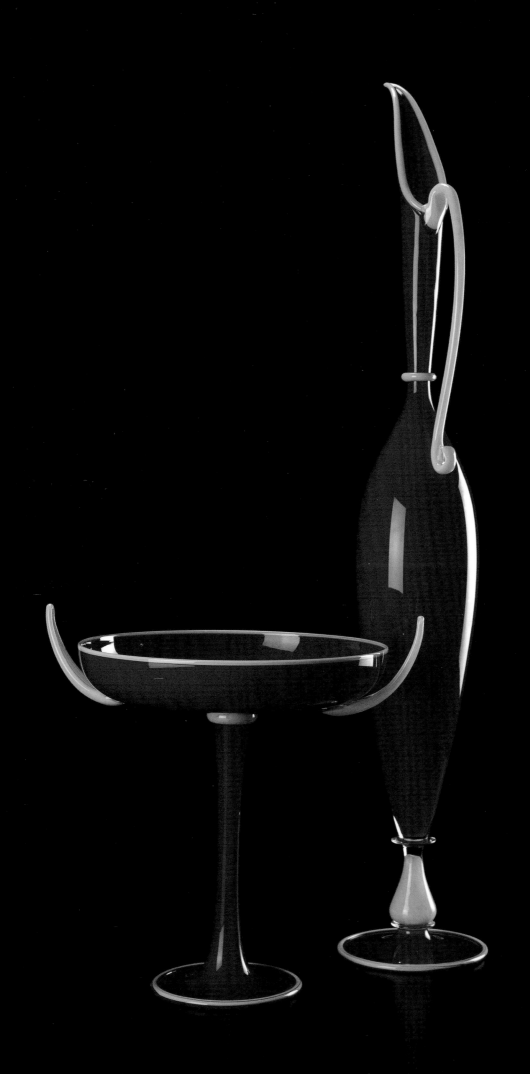

Red and Yellow Pair
1997
greatest h. 36 inches

Yellow and Orange Pair
1997
greatest h. 34 inches

Orange and Chartreuse Trio
1999
greatest h. 40 inches

I am constantly having ideas for new forms, and there are a lot of
things that I want to do that are technically beyond me. I
have to convince myself that a form can be made, and then
I just keep working at it until I get it.

New Blue
Needlenose Pair
1996
greatest h. 39 inches

Someone once asked me how I developed my color sensibility, and I said that it was sort of a reaction to all of the surface decoration I'd grown up around. It was, like, none of that ever spoke to me. But a big, giant, blue vase worked.

PRECEDING
SPREAD

Chartreuse
Needlenose Pair
1995
greatest h. 33 inches

Ivory
Needlenose Pair
1997
greatest h. 41 inches

Veronese Vase and
Colored Cups
1999
greatest h. 10 inches

Queen Margherita
Goblets
1999
greatest h. 8½ inches

Lino Tagliapietra once told me that if I made goblets for seven years, I could make anything. Goblets are about figuring things out, working through form, and through the repetition, developing skill.

Cup Box
1997
14 × 12 × 12 inches

Cup Shelf
1999
96 × 24 inches

Yellow Trio
1999
greatest h. 39½ inches

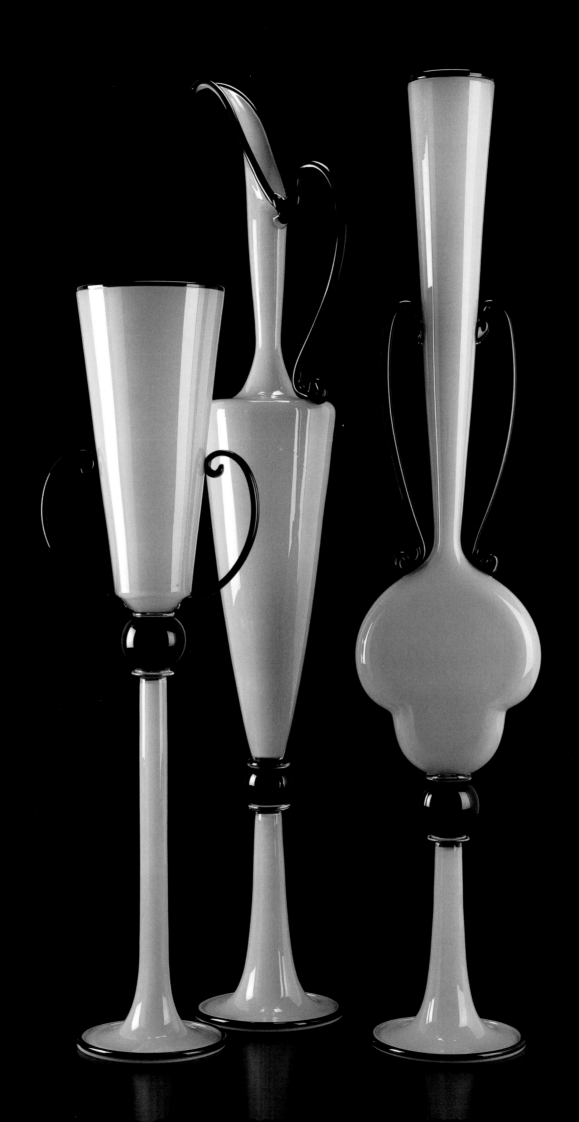

Black and Blue Pair
1998
greatest h. 40 inches

Moss Green Trio
1999
greatest h. 40½ inches

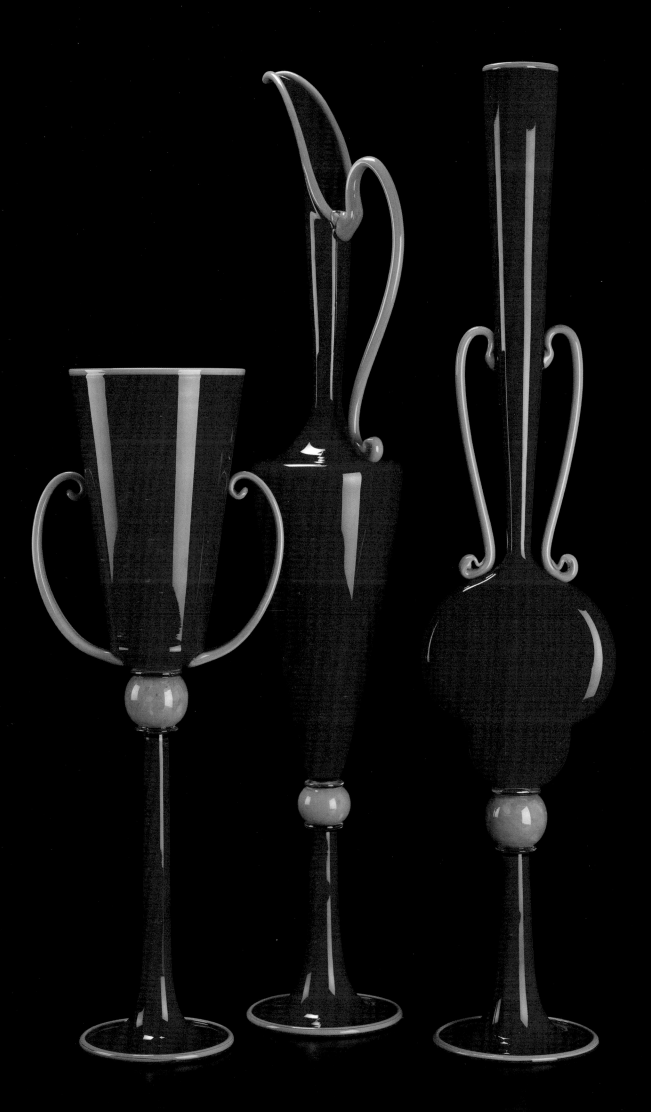

Red Pair
1998
greatest h. 40½ inches

I go shopping for color bars and I buy what jumps out at me. I
don't go with a plan; I just think certain colors look good.
It's like buying vegetables. I'll think, "That blue looks especially good, I'll buy some of that," or, "This black is extra
dark." And I put it together from there. It's the quality of a
color that I find most appealing.

When I get them right, the *Mosaics* are my favorite things to make. These objects came out of the interest that Dick Marquis and I share in the work of the Italian architect and glass designer Carlo Scarpa.

Mosaic Vase, Red in Yellow
1999
36 × 8 inches

The making of this vase is shown in
the sequence of working photographs,
pages 141–47.

Mosaic Vases, Tiger Motif
1997
greatest h. 36 inches

Mosaic Vase, Black in Yellow
1999
40 × 8 inches

Mosaic Vase, White Dots
1998
35 × 8 inches

PRECEDING
SPREAD

detail
Mosaic Vase, Red
Postage Stamp
1999
36 × 8½ inches

Mosaic Vase, White
1999
38 × 8 inches

Mosaic Vase, Yellow Kiwi
1999
40 × 8 inches

Green Mosaic Vase
2000
37 × 8 inches

Mosaic Vase, Red and Black
1999
40 × 8 inches

When I am working at the bench, making a form, nothing else
matters to me at that moment. When I make a shape that
goes well, I feel it through my hands, and that's very satis-
fying. That's a lot of why I make the things I make. It
doesn't always feel good—there are bad days too. But on a
good day, when it's going well, it's a great thing, and a really
powerful motivator for me.

detail
Mosaic Vase, Yellow Postage Stamp
1999
36 × 8 inches

detail
Mosaic Vases, Orange with Blue
1997
greatest h. 35 inches

116

detail
Mosaic Vases, Orange with Blue
1997
greatest h. 35 inches

Mosaic Vases. Yellow
1997
greatest h. 35 inches

Mosaic Vases. Yellow
1997
greatest h. 35 inches

PRECEDING
SPREAD

Mosaic Vase. Red and
Yellow with Blue
1998
34 × 8 inches

detail
Mosaic Vase. Red and
Yellow with Blue

detail
**Mosaic Vase,
Red in Yellow
with Yellow**
1999
$37 \times 8\frac{1}{2}$ inches

Mosaic Vase, Yellow in Red
1999
$38\frac{1}{2} \times 8$ inches

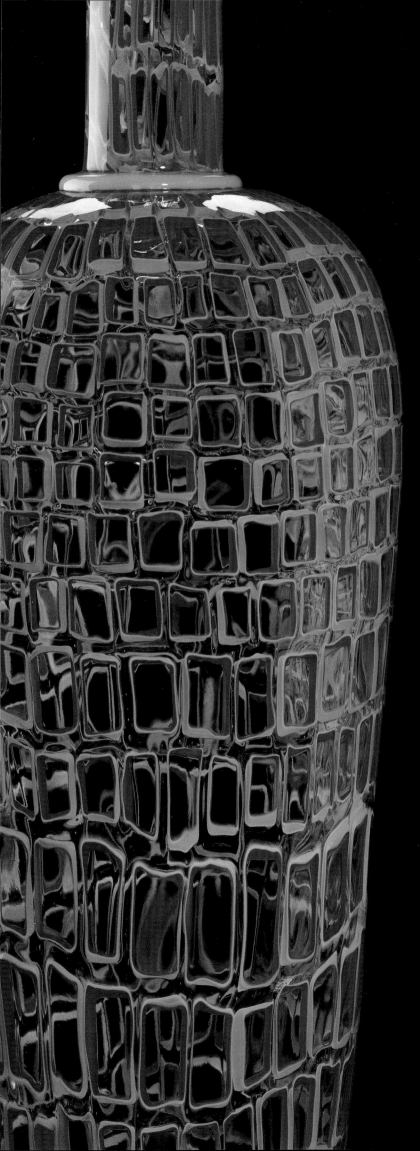

I wanted to make a piece that had stripes, straight parallel lines, coming down from the neck to the shoulder. It proved to be difficult to keep the lines straight enough to satisfy my vision. So I started making the *Finestras* with a mosaic shoulder. *Finestra* means "window," and I gave the vases that name because the shoulders were transparent.

Finestra Vase, Yellow with Black
and Yellow Mosaic
1999
40½ × 8 inches

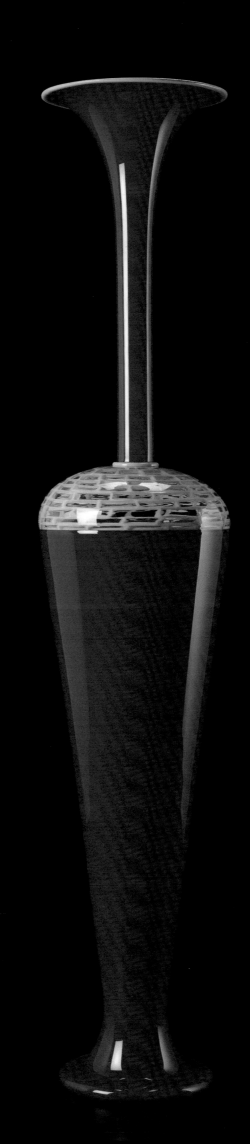

Finestra Vase, Red
with Yellow Mosaic
1999
39 × 9 inches

Finestra Vase, Yellow
with Orange Stripe
1999
39½ × 9 inches

detail
Finestra Vase with Yellow Fusilli

Finestra Vase with Yellow Fusilli
2000
39 × 7 inches

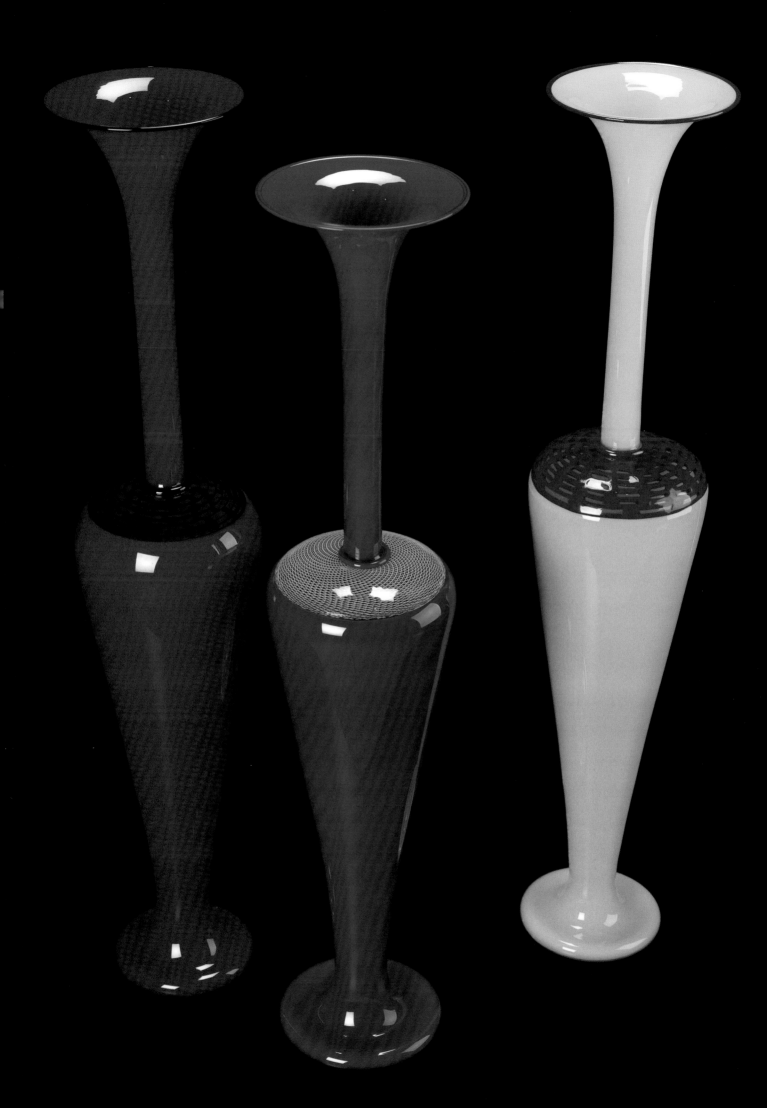

I also make the *Finestras* with *reticello,* a net glass with air bubbles—a super-fussy, very exacting Italian technique. This past summer, Lino Tagliapietra was at Pilchuck, and I learned how to make the *reticello* from him. It's technically challenging, and then of course I have to apply it to something original.

Finestra Vase Pair, Red and
Yellow with Reticello
1999
greatest h. 39 inches

Finestra Vases, Yellow and Yellow
Reticello and Red Interior
2000
greatest h. 41 inches

▶

Finestra Vase, Red
with Yellow
Reticello
2000
41 × 7½ inches

detail
**Finestra Vase, Black with
Yellow and Black Reticello**
1999
38 × 8 inches

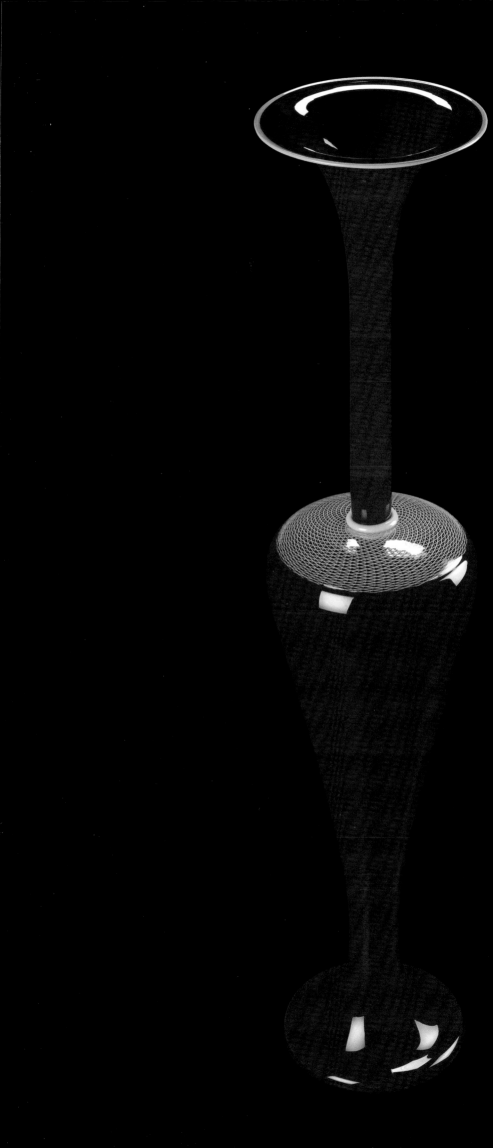

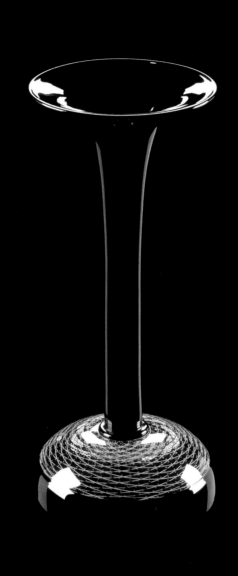

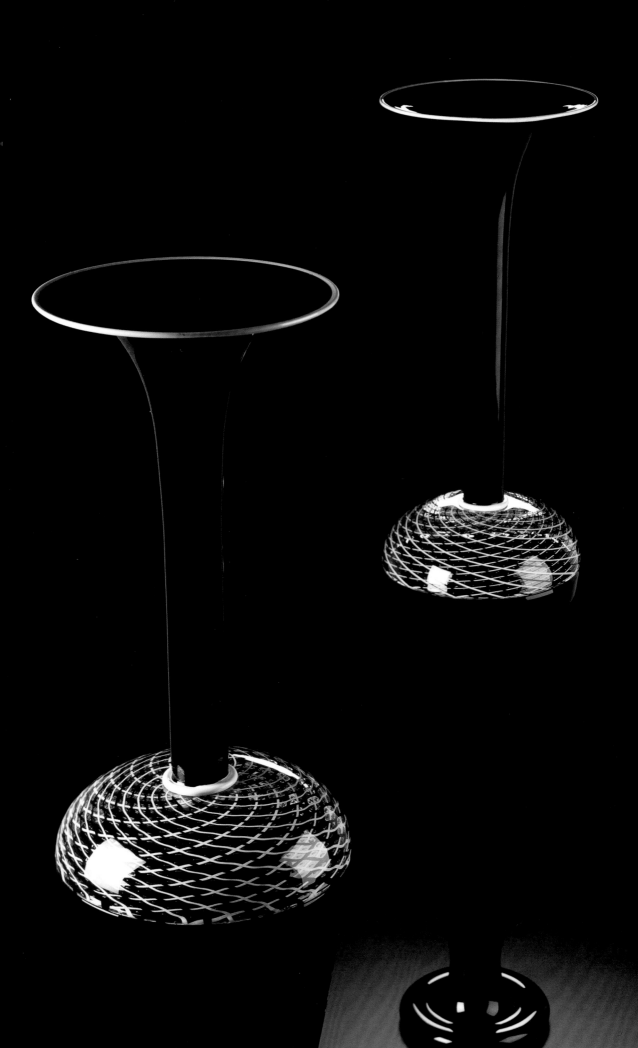

MAKING A MOSAIC VASE, 1999

Dante Marioni and his team—Paul Cunningham, Nadege Desgenetez, Robbie Miller, Janusz Posniak, and Preston Singletary—work at Benjamin Moore's studio in Seattle.

To make a *murrine*, or
mosaic, vase, clear glass
is first gathered and then
rolled in colored glass
chips.

On the marver, the hot
glass is formed into a
rectangle.

The glass is then reheated
and hung from a ladder
to make a *murrine* cane.
Janusz Posniak stretches
the hot glass to the floor.

After the *murrine* cane has
cooled, it is chopped into
pieces by Robbie Miller.
The *murrine* pieces that
will form the body of the
vase are then carefully
arranged into a pattern on
a large metal plate.

The *murrine* pieces that
will form the neck of
the vase are arranged on
a separate, smaller metal
plate.

This plate is heated at
2200 degrees Fahrenheit
until the glass is molten.

In the meantime, I have made a glass "wheel" on the end of a blowpipe.

The *murrine* glass pattern is rolled onto the wheel.

The cylinder is then carefully closed. This will become the neck of the vase.

The vase neck is then heated and rolled repeatedly on the marver. The glass wheel for the vase body is visible in the foreground.

The neck of the vase takes shape.

A small wrap is applied to one end of the neck.

The large plate is ready to be heated.

Paul Cunningham rolls the large *murrine* pattern onto his blowpipe. This will become the body of the vase.

Then Paul and Janusz close it up, forming a cylinder.

It takes a while.

The *murrine* cylinder is plugged with clear glass. Now it's a bubble.

The bubble has been carefully heated and marvered before it is brought over to the bench to be inflated. Nadege Desgenetez works with Paul and me.

The inflated bubble is hot.

The vase body takes shape.

A wrap is applied to the bottom, or foot, of the vase.

The vase is transferred from the blowpipe to the punty by Preston Singletary.

As the body of the vase reheats, I check the size of the neck.

Both pieces of the vase—the neck and the body—are reheated prior to being joined.

The joining is the hardest part.

Once the two pieces are joined, Robbie blows into the blowpipe to ensure a seal.

Then the vase goes back into the fire.

A wrap is applied to the top, or lip, of the vase.

I open the mouth of the vase as Preston turns the pipe at the bench.

Nadege heats the punty with a torch while I work on the mouth of the vase.

The vase must be reheated about every thirty seconds.

Now the vase takes its final shape.

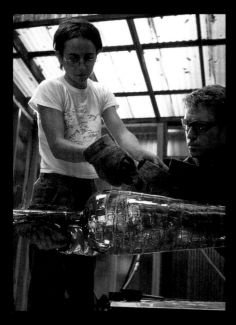

Last adjustments are made to make sure the vase is straight and on center.

The vase goes into the fire for the last time.

The vase is knocked off the pipe, and Robbie loads it into the annealing oven, where it will gradually cool down for twenty-four hours.

Bear, the cat.

Acknowledgments

I would like to acknowledge the people who have assisted and inspired me so far—my wife and best friend Alison, who helped put this book together, and my dad, Paul, for everything. Richard Marquis, Benjamin Moore, Lino Tagliapietra, and my uncle, Joseph Marioni, have been good friends and positive role models.

A lot of different people have helped me over the years in the studio, and I want to thank everyone for making it happen. Many people don't realize that glassblowing requires a team effort. To do it well, you need to have an environment that is happy and friendly. This is best achieved by assembling a group of friends—people who get along, who are happy and positive. Humor helps too. I have been so fortunate throughout my career that some of these people happened to be my closest friends—a few of them since we were kids, even before we wanted to be glassblowers. I have never for a moment considered anything else but this fact to be the single most rewarding aspect of this profession, and this work could never have happened without them: Joey DeCamp, Paul Cunningham, Robbie Miller, Benjamin Moore, Preston Singletary, and Janusz Pozniak.

DANTE MARIONI

Selected Public Collections

Birmingham Museum, Birmingham, Alabama

The Carnegie Museum of Art, Pittsburgh

Chrysler Museum, Norfolk, Virginia

Cincinnati Museum of Art, Cincinnati

Columbia Museum of Art, Columbia, South Carolina

The Corning Museum of Glass, Corning, New York

Davis Wright & Jones, Seattle and Bellevue, Washington

Hunter Museum, Chattanooga, Tennessee

Huntsville Museum, Huntsville, Alabama

Japanese National Museum of Craft, Tokyo

The Los Angeles County Museum of Art, Los Angeles

MCI, Washington, D.C.

Microsoft Corporation, Redmond, Washington

Mint Museum of Craft and Design, Charlotte, North Carolina

National Gallery of Victoria, Melbourne, Australia

National Museum of Art, Renwick Gallery, Smithsonian Institution,
    Washington, D.C.

New Zealand National Museum, Auckland, New Zealand

The Powerhouse Museum, Sydney, Australia

The Prescott Collection of Pilchuck Glass at the U.S. Bank Centre,
    Seattle

Safeco Insurance Company, Seattle

Security Pacific Bank, Seattle

University Art Museum, Arizona State University, Tempe

Vero Beach Museum, Vero Beach, Florida

The White House Crafts Collection, Washington, D.C.

Yokohama Museum of Art, Yokohama, Japan

List of Plates

All photographs by Roger Schreiber
unless otherwise noted.

Page 6: *Yellow and Red Pair*, 1998. Greatest h. 40 in.
Collection of Alex and Norma Cugini.

Page 8: Detail, *Leaf Vases* (see page 51)

Page 10: *Red Needlenose Pair*, 1996. Greatest h. 38½ in.
Collection of Beverly and Jerry Rashbaum.

Page 17: *Purple and Chartreuse Gambo Vases*, 1997.
Greatest h. 40 in. Private collection.

Page 18: Detail, *Finestra Vase, Black with Yellow and Black
Reticello*, 1999. 38 × 8 in. Collection of the artist.

Pages 42–43: *Colored Cups*, 1994. Greatest h. 8 in. Private
collection.

Page 44: *Whopper Vases*, 1992. Greatest h. 27 in. Private
collection.

Page 45: *Whopper Vases*, 1993. Greatest h. 29 in. Red with
Yellow, private collection; Blue with Red, collection of
Andrew Davis.

Page 46: *Whopper Vases*, 1992. Greatest h. 27 in. Private
collection.

Page 48: *Chartreuse Etruscan Pair*, 1989. Greatest h. 37 in.
Private collection.

Page 49: *Etruscan Vase Forms*, 1989. Greatest h. 36 in.
Collection of the artist.

Page 51: *Leaf Vases*, 1996. Greatest h. 44 in. Private
collection.

Page 52: *Leaf Vases*, 1998. Greatest h. 45 in. Collection of
Anthony Biancaniello.

Page 53: *Leaf Vases*, 1997. Greatest h. 44 in. Private
collection.

Page 55: *Chartreuse Pair*, 1992. Greatest h. 32 in. Collection
of Mr. and Mrs. William Block.

Page 56: *Orange Pair*, 1992. Greatest h. 32 in. Collection of
the artist.

Page 57: *Red Pair*, 1992. Greatest h. 33 in. Collection of the
artist.

Page 58: *Red and Yellow Gambo Vases*, 1998. Greatest
h. 41 in. Collection of the artist.

Page 59: *Yellow with Black Gambo Vase*, 1998. 40 × 8 in.
Private collection.

Page 61: *Gambo Vases*, 1998. Greatest h. 39 in. Private
collection.

Pages 62–63: Detail, *Gambo Vase* (see page 61).

Page 64: *Blue and Red Gambo Vase*, 1998. 39 × 8½ in.
Collection of the artist.

Page 65: *Rhubarb and Milfoil Gambo Vases*, 1996. Greatest
h. 35½ in. Collection of James and Maisie Houghton.

Page 67: *Black and White Gambo Vase*, 2000, 41 × 6 in.
Collection of the artist.

Page 68: *Black and Green Flask*, 1998. 48 × 8 in. Collection of the artist.

Page 69: *Pea Green Pair*, 1999. Greatest h. 39 in. Collection
of the artist.

Page 70: *Chartreuse and Orange Trio*, 1999. Greatest
h. 40 in. Private collection.

Page 71: *Chartreuse and Orange Pair*, 1996. Greatest
h. 38½ in. Private collection.

Page 73: *Flask Pair*, 1996. Greatest h. 40 in. Private
collection.

Page 75: *New Blue Trio*, 1997. Greatest h. 34 in. Private
collection.

Page 76: *Ivory Pair*, 1996. Greatest h. 35 in. Collection of
the Powerhouse Museum, Sydney, Australia.

Page 77: *Black Trio*, 1996. Greatest h. 38 in. Private collection. Photo by Rob Vinnedge.

Page 78: *Oxblood Flask*, 1998. 50 × 8 in. Private collection.

Page 79: *Pea Green Trio*, 1998. Greatest h. 36 in. Collection
of the artist.

Page 80: *Red and Yellow Pair*, 1997. Greatest h. 36 in.
Collection of Mr. and Mrs. Martin Lutin.

Page 81: *Yellow and Orange Pair*, 1997. Greatest h. 34 in.
Collection of the artist.

Page 82: *Orange and Chartreuse Trio*, 1999. Greatest
h. 40 in. Collection of Michael and Melanie Traub.

Page 83: *Green Needlenose Pair*, 1997. Greatest h. 41 in.
Collection of Barrie Mowatt.

Page 84: *Chartreuse Needlenose Pair*, 1995. Greatest
h. 33 in. Collection of the artist.

Biography

Born March 3, 1964, Mill Valley, California

EDUCATION
Pilchuck Glass School, Stanwood, Washington
Colorado Mountain College, Vail, Colorado
Penland School of Crafts, Penland, North Carolina

SELECTED SOLO EXHIBITIONS

1999
Howard Yezerski Gallery, Boston
Marx Saunders Gallery, Chicago
Susan Duval Gallery, Aspen, Colorado
William Traver Gallery, Seattle

1998
Maurine Littleton Gallery, Washington, D.C.
Riley Hawk Gallery, Cleveland
Riley Hawk Gallery, Columbus, Ohio
Leedy Voulkos, Kansas City, Missouri
Howard Yezerski Gallery, Boston

1997
Contemporary Art Niki, Tokyo
Galleria Marina Barovier, Venice
William Traver Gallery, Seattle

1996
Heller Gallery, New York

1995
Grand Central Gallery, Tampa
William Traver Gallery, Seattle
Margo Jacobsen Gallery, Portland, Oregon

1994
Marta Hewett Gallery, Cincinnati
Gallery Nakama, Tokyo
Heller Gallery, New York

1993
Connell Gallery, Atlanta
Robert Lehman Gallery, New York Experimental
    Glass Workshop, Brooklyn

William Traver Gallery, Seattle
Kate Elliott/Betsy Rosenfield, Chicago International
    New Art Forms Expo at Navy Pier, Chicago

1992
Betsy Rosenfield Gallery, Chicago
Marta Hewett Gallery, Cincinnati

1991
William Traver Gallery, Seattle
Grohe Gallery, Boston

1990
Studio 5 Seibu, Tokyo

1989
Traver/Sutton Gallery, Seattle

1987
Traver/Sutton Gallery, Seattle

SELECTED GROUP EXHIBITIONS

1999
Global Art Triennial, Olandstryckarna, Borgholm, Sweden
Ellen Noel Art Museum, Odessa, Texas
Grand Central Gallery, Tampa
Influences in Contemporary Glass, Sea-Tac International
    Airport, Seattle

1998
Venezia Aperto Vetro, Venice
Galleria Marina Barovier, Venice
Marioni/Marioni, Fresno Art Museum, Fresno, California
Buschlen/Mowatt Fine Arts, Vancouver, B.C., Canada

1997
Imago Gallery, Palm Desert, California
Cleveland Museum of Art, Cleveland
Heller Gallery, Sculpture Objects Functional Art (SOFA)
    Expo, Miami
Mano Volante, Etherton Gallery, Tucson
Raucous Color, Penland School of Crafts Gallery, Penland,
    North Carolina
Heir Apparent: Translating the Secrets of Venetian Glass,
    Bellevue Art Museum, Bellevue, Washington

Glass Today by American Studio Artists, Museum of
Fine Arts, Boston

Concept Art Gallery, Pittsburgh

Heller Gallery, Sculpture Objects Functional Art (SOFA)
Expo, Chicago

Embracing Beauty, Huntsville Museum, Huntsville,
Alabama

1996

Murrine Storia, Elliott Brown Gallery, Seattle

William Traver Gallery, Sculpture Objects Functional Art
(SOFA) Expo, Chicago

Jerald Melberg Gallery, Charlotte, North Carolina

Susan Duvall Gallery, Aspen, Colorado

Connell Gallery, Atlanta

Riley Hawk Gallery, Columbus, Ohio

1995

Holding the Past: Historicism in Northwest Glass Sculpture,
Seattle Art Museum, Seattle

1993

Formed by Fire, Carnegie Museum of Art, Pittsburgh

Benjamin Moore and Dante Marioni, Buschlen/Mowatt
Fine Arts, Vancouver, B.C., Canada

Dante Marioni and Benjamin Moore, Margo Jacobsen
Gallery, Portland, Oregon

Out of the Fire, Contemporary Art Niki, Tokyo

Collectibles, LewAllen Gallery, Santa Fe

1992

Kate Elliott Contemporary Glass, Chicago International
New Art Forms Expo at Navy Pier, Chicago

Clearly Art: Pilchuck's Glass Legacy, Whatcom Museum of
History, Bellingham, Washington (toured United States
through 1995)

100 Goblets, Gallery Nakama, Tokyo

Modern Glass, Cone/Solow Gallery, Mendocino, California

Glass '92, Imago Gallery, Palm Springs, California

LewAllen Gallery, Santa Fe

Artists from Pilchuck Glass School, Sea-Tac International
Airport, Seattle

Buschlen/Mowatt Fine Arts, Vancouver, B.C., Canada

1991

Le Verre Contemporain, Civic Centre, Rouen, France

Elaine Horwitch Gallery, Scottsdale, Arizona

Northwest Glass, LewAllen Gallery, Santa Fe

Glass America, Heller Gallery, New York

Pilchuck Glass, Bellevue Art Museum, Bellevue,
Washington

1990

American Glass, Gallery Nakama, Tokyo

Vessels, American Craft Museum, New York

1989

Craft Today USA, American Craft Museum, New York
(toured Europe through 1992)

1988

Pilchuck School: The Great Northwest Glass Experiment,
Bellevue Art Museum, Bellevue, Washington

Pilchuck Glass Artists of the American Northwest, American
Embassy, Prague

Young Americans, American Craft Museum, New York

1987

Beaver Gallery, Canberra, Australia

Traver/Sutton Gallery, Seattle

Northwest Glass, Philbrook Art Center, Tulsa

1986

Symmetry in Contemporary Glass, Traver/Sutton Gallery,
Seattle

1985

Mandarin Gallery, Tacoma, Washington

1984

Greenwood Gallery, Seattle

1983

American Glass Now, Yamaha Corporation, Tokyo

TEACHING EXPERIENCE

1990–1998

Instructor, Pilchuck Glass School, Stanwood, Washington

1996

Instructor, SUWA Glass Museum, Nagano, Japan

1994

Instructor with Lino Tagliapietra, Haystack Mountain
School of Arts & Crafts, Deer Isle, Maine

Penland School of Crafts, Penland, North Carolina

1993

Rhode Island School of Design, Providence

Toyama Glass Art Institute, Toyama City, Japan

Instructor with Lino Tagliapietra, Pilchuck Glass School,
Stanwood, Washington

1989–1992

Instructor, Niijima Glass Art Center, Niijima, Japan

1992

Instructor with Lino Tagliapietra, Haystack Mountain
School of Arts & Crafts, Deer Isle, Maine

Visiting artist with Richard Marquis, University of Hawaii,
Honolulu

1991

Instructor with Paul Marioni, Haystack Mountain
School of Arts & Crafts, Deer Isle, Maine

1990

Fujikawa Craft Park, Fujikawa, Japan

1989

Wanganui Summer School, Wanganui, New Zealand

1988

Penland School of Crafts, Penland, North Carolina

1987

Guest instructor, Canberra School of Art, Canberra,
Australia

Assistant to Richard Marquis, Haystack Mountain
School of Arts & Crafts, Deer Isle, Maine

Assistant to Lino Tagliapietra and Benjamin Moore,
Pilchuck Glass School, Stanwood, Washington

1985

Instructor, Pratt Fine Arts Center, Seattle

AWARDS

1997

"Outstanding Achievement in Glass," UrbanGlass Award,
Brooklyn

1988

"Young Americans," American Craft Museum, New York

1987

Louis Comfort Tiffany Foundation Award

1985

The Glass Eye Scholarship, Seattle

SELECTED BIBLIOGRAPHY

American Library Association. *Booklist*, October 15, 1995,
cover.

Anderson, Nola. "Anatomy of the Vessel." *Craft Arts*,
October/December 1987, pp. 71–74. First published
in *Canberra Times*, March 15, 1987.

"Art That Pulls Its Weight at Safeco." *Financial Executive*,
November/December 1991.

Beauty of Contemporary Glass. Tokyo: Sekisho Shoji
Company, 1991.

Chambers, Karen. "The White House Collection." *Neues
Glas*, winter 1996, pp. 46–49.

"Contemporary Art Glass Movement." *Glass and Art*,
spring 1993, pp. 25–35 and cover.

"Dante Marioni, Seattle's Standard Bearer." *Glass and Art*,
winter 1997, pp. 14–44 and cover.

Elle Decor, December 1991/January 1992, p. 26.

Hackett, Regina. "Father and Son Put Different Varieties
of Pop into Glass Art." *Seattle Post-Intelligencer*,
May 31, 1992.

Hackett, Regina. "First in His Glass." *Seattle Post-
Intelligencer*, May 23, 1995.

Hackett, Regina. "Rhythm and Hues in Glass." *Seattle
Post-Intelligencer*, May 15, 1999.

Hammell, Lisa. "Young Americans 1988." *American Craft*,
December 1988/January 1989, pp. 42–49.

Herman, Lloyd. *Clearly Art: Pilchuck's Glass Legacy*.
Bellingham, Washington: Whatcom Museum of History
and Art, 1992, p. 46.

"Hot Glass." *Town and Country Magazine*, December 1996,
p. 71.

Kangas, Matthew. "Dante Marioni: Apprentice to
Tradition." *American Craft*, February/March 1994,
pp. 34–37 and cover.

Kuroki, Rika. "Interview with Dante Marioni." *Glass Works*,
January 1990, pp. 60–61.

Miller, Bonnie. *Out of the Fire: Contemporary Glass Artists
and Their Work*. San Francisco: Chronicle Books, 1991,
pp. 60–63.

Monroe, Michael W., and John Bigelow Taylor. *The White
House Collection of American Crafts*. New York: Harry N.
Abrams, 1995, p. 44 and front and back cover.

Patton, Phil. "Today's Crafts Join Our Nation's Past at the
White House." *Smithsonian*, June 1995, pp. 52–57 and
cover.

Puget Sound Business Journal, December 8–14, 1995,
pp. 1, 39.

Roseman, Janet, and John Clayton. *Gump's Since 1861: A
San Francisco Legend*. San Francisco: Chronicle Books,
1991, pp. 72–73.

Tarzan-Ament, Dolores. "Dante Marioni." *Seattle Times*,
February 15, 1987.

Waggoner, Shawn. "Dante Marioni: Upholding the Vessel
Tradition." *Glass Art*, winter 1994, pp. 4–8.

Wichert, Geoff. "Dante Marioni." *Glass*, spring 1998, p. 49.

Wichert, Geoff. "Dante Marioni." *Vetro*, October/December
1999, pp. 22–27.

Index

Numbers in *italic type* refer to pages with illustrations.

About the Contributors

TINA OLDKNOW is an art historian specializing in contemporary glass. An expert in the field of ancient Greek and Roman art, Oldknow began her glass studies with the vessels of classical antiquity. While working as a curator at the Los Angeles County Museum of Art in the 1980s, she was introduced to contemporary studio glass, an interest that grew after she moved to the Pacific Northwest. Oldknow is the editor of the *Glass Art Society Journal* and author of *Pilchuck: A Glass School* (1996), *Chihuly Persians* (1996), and *Richard Marquis Objects* (1997). In February 2000, Oldknow was appointed Curator of Modern Glass at The Corning Museum of Glass, Corning, New York.

JOSEPH MARIONI is The Painter. The Painter, who studied at the Cincinnati Art Academy and San Francisco Art Institute, has lived in New York since 1972. He is internationally recognized for his work as a high modernist painter and has had museum exhibitions throughout Europe and the United States. He has lectured on modernist painting and the radical concrete on both continents, and has twice been invited as artist-in-residence at the Pilchuck Glass School in Stanwood, Washington.

EDWARD R. QUICK is Curator, Presidential Materials Staff, of the National Archives and Records Administration in Washington, D.C. The *White House Collection of American Crafts* exhibition, which he travels, includes Dante Marioni's *Yellow Pair* (1993). Quick is former director of the Sheldon Swope Art Museum and the Berman Museum and is founding curator of the William Jefferson Clinton Presidential Library and Museum that will be established in Little Rock, Arkansas.

ROGER SCHREIBER has worked as a Seattle-based photographer for more than twenty years. While his speciality is environmental portraiture, he has concentrated professionally in photographing three-dimensional art for artists' portfolios and publication. He regularly conducts workshops for artists on how to photograph their own work. Schreiber's photographs have appeared in numerous books and arts and life-style magazines.

RUSSELL JOHNSON is a Seattle-based freelance photographer. His projects range from a book on a sacred mountain in Tibet to numerous assignments around the world for artists working with glass. Johnson has photographed many well-known artists at work in the studio in addition to photographing their artwork. His photographs have appeared in national and international exhibition catalogues, books, and magazines.

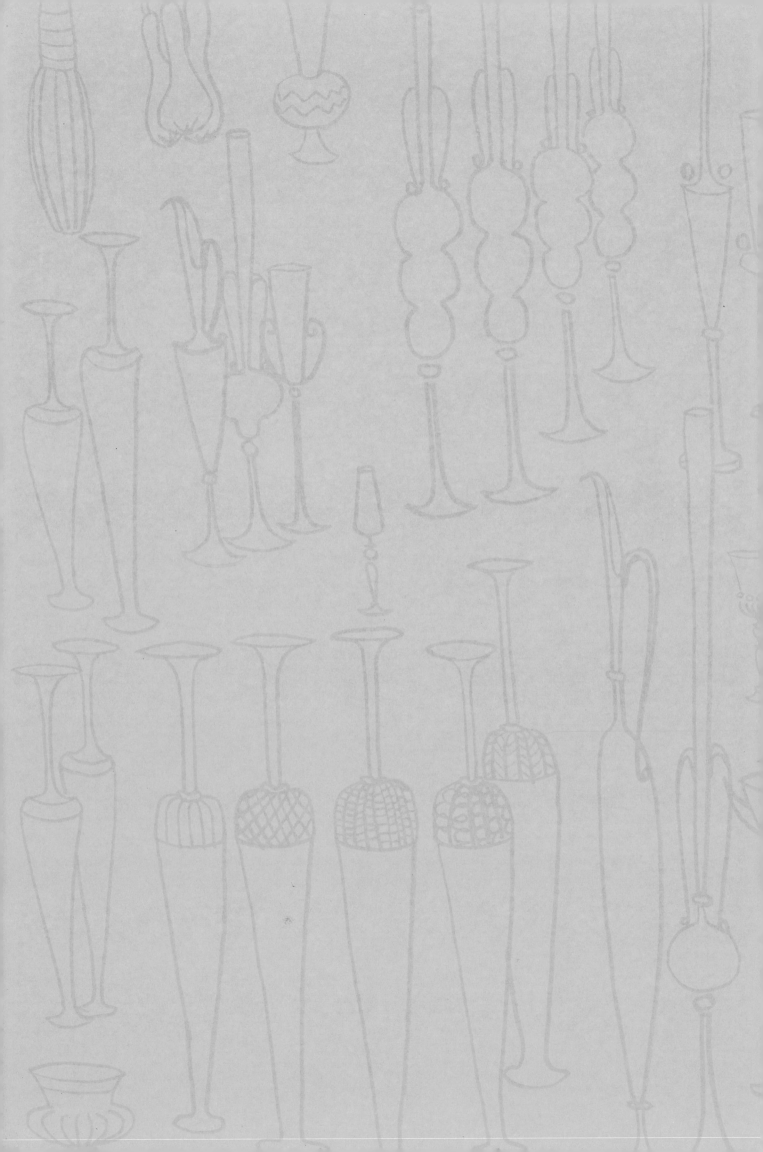